The Betrayal of the Constitution

How Dishonest Judges Have Undermined the "Rule of Law"

By Stephen Erwin

DEDICATION

Dedicated to my best friend "Sue", whose adventures in the courts taught me more about the Civil and Criminal Injustice system than I ever wanted to know.

And

To Judge Robert Bork, whose outstanding book "The Tempting of America" should be a wakeup call to anyone seeking real justice in America, and required reading in every high school and college.

And

To Glen Beck, who will need at least three full rolls of Duct Tape if he ever tries to read this book.

CONTENTS

INTRODUCTION
The Supreme Court Only Has One Wing - A Left Wing

It is the goal of this book to expose the corruption of our legal system and the deconstruction of our Constitution in a condensed and easy to read manner that avoids the legalese of the lawyers and enshrined BS of the politicians.

This book is based on one simple premise. **THE ONLY IMPARTIAL, NEUTRAL, MODERATE, CENTRIST POSITION ON THE LAW IS THAT IT ACTUALLY MEANS WHAT IT SAYS.** This is what the Founders intended and it is what the vast majority of the citizens of the United States foolishly believe is still true.

On this basis every Justice on the current United States Supreme Court is to the left of center including the most impartial and honest Supreme Court Justice Clarence Thomas.

You Can't Fix Stupid. Fortunately Americans aren't stupid, but far too many are left totally ignorant about the judiciary by our educational system. It is only by exposing the dishonesty and lack of integrity that is epidemic in our Courts that we have any hope of regaining our true rights under the Constitution of the United States that the Supreme Court of those United States has Betrayed

CHAPTER 1. - A REPUBLIC, IF YOU CAN KEEP IT

The great American patriot Benjamin Franklin, upon leaving the Constitutional Convention in Philadelphia in 1787, was asked what form of government the United States was going to have. Without hesitation he answered "A Republic, if you can keep it."

As many times as you may have been told that the United States is a democracy, the word is nowhere to be found in our Declaration of Independence or Constitution. Our Founding Fathers were students of history and worked hard to develop a form of government that would not repeat the mistakes of the past. History had proved to them that democracy was perhaps the worst form of government.

"We are a Republican Government. Real liberty is never found in despotism or in the extremes of Democracy.... It has been observed that a pure democracy if it were practicable would be the most perfect government. Experience has proved that no position is more false than this. The ancient democracies in which the people themselves deliberated never possessed one good feature of government. Their very character was tyranny; their figure deformity." - Alexander Hamilton

"Democracy never lasts long. It soon wastes, exhausts, and murders itself. There never was a democracy yet that did not commit suicide." - John Adams

"Democracies have ever been spectacles of turbulence and contention; have ever been found incompatible with personal security or the rights of property; and have in general been as short in their lives as they have been violent in their death. - James Madison

"The experience of all former ages had shown that of all human governments, democracy was the most unstable, fluctuating and short-lived." - John Quincy Adams

By democracy they are referring to simple majority rule. If fifty one percent of the population wants something then that becomes the law. It is a simple prescription for mob rule and the swift destruction of the rights of the minority. The Founders themselves explain it much better than my own words ever could.

"A democracy is nothing more than mob rule, where fifty-one percent of the people may take away the rights of the other forty-nine." - Thomas Jefferson

"Democracy is two wolves and a lamb voting on what to have for lunch. Liberty is a well-armed lamb contesting the vote!" - Benjamin Franklin

"The democracy will cease to exist when you take away from those who are willing to work and give to those who would not." - Thomas Jefferson

So what is this Republic that Franklin feels is so superior to democracy. The definition of Republic is:

1. A state in which the supreme power rests in the body of citizens entitled to vote and is exercised by representatives chosen directly or indirectly by them.

2. A state in which the head of government is not a monarch or other hereditary head of state.

Of course this simple definition was not the "Republic" Franklin was referring to. Franklin's was a Constitutional Republic that was created and approved by the People through their representatives and which provided specific rules for the government to follow, enumerated specific rights for the people, and provided checks and balances to keep any individual or branch of government from gaining too much power.

All of this was spelled out in the Constitution of the United States of America. There were three co-equal branches of Government. They were the Legislative, Executive, and Judicial. Unfortunately we now have two sort of maybe co-equal branches both subject to the dictates of the Judicial Branch. And we have a lazy legislative branch that has allowed the executive branch to write 165,000 pages of rules that have the force of legislation and to engage in wars without a Declaration of War.

The legislature was divided into Two Branches, the House of Representatives which represented the People and the Senate which represented the interests of the States. To this end the House was elected by popular vote and the Senate was "chosen by the Legislature thereof (The State)." The number of representatives was set by the population of the State and the Senate had two members per state so that the large states could not run roughshod over the small ones. Unfortunately we were fooled into taking the Senate away from the State legislatures and giving it to the people in the name of Democracy when we ratified the 17th Amendment. This removed the best protection we had for States rights which in turn protected us from the central government becoming all powerful. The Jury System and a Jury's right to nullify a law they thought was unjust was another check on the powers of government. Unfortunately Judges today routinely ban lawyers from telling juries that they have this right.

Only allowing property owners the right to vote was perceived as a check on the majority levying confiscatory taxes on property owners. This is another check we gave away in the name of democracy. It has led to nearly half the population receiving government handouts instead of paying income taxes.

In the UK they would seem to have a very similar form of republican government, but in fact their republic is actually a representative democracy. They have their Magna Carta which defines the rights of the people, but it only applies to the King and, because it was written by the legislature, it can be changed by the legislature. This may explain why the Fascist economic model has taken root faster in England than America.

Because our Constitution came from the People it binds our leaders by the "RULE OF LAW", but only if we revolt (peaceably at the ballot box) and force them to comply with the Constitution that most in our government no longer either read or understand.

Fascism was originally a liberal progressive economic model invented by Mussolini, adopted by Hitler, and praised by the left through the early thirties until it became overly nationalistic, militaristic, dictatorial, and started killing people. Then those attributes of evil suddenly became the definition of what was now called a far right movement. In this economic model a government of elite leaders controls business, but does not own it. Think ObamaCare, EPA, Dodd Frank, the Tax Code, and those 165,000 pages of regulations that were never passed by Congress or signed by the president. Under this model, if the government controls work as planned, the politicians can take the credit and, if they are a disaster, it is the fault of the greedy corporations. You "gotta love" politicians.

CHAPTER 2. - THE RULE OF LAW - WORDS HAVE MEANING

John Adams said, "No man will contend that a nation can be free that is not governed by fixed laws. All other government than that of permanent known laws is the government of mere will and pleasure." Adams would have understood why the Obama recovery was the worst since the great depression.

Austrian philosopher and economist Frederick A. Hayek defined the phrase the "Rule of Law" to mean that "government in all its actions is bound by rules fixed and announced beforehand—rules which make it possible to foresee with fair certainty how the authority will use its coercive powers in given circumstances and to plan one's individual affairs on the basis of this knowledge." Obama and his allies in Congress have created an environment with no certainty whatsoever.

Most economists will agree that the "Rule of Law" fosters economic activity by protecting property rights. A legal system that clearly allocates and protects property rights from infringement by the state or others promotes economic development and is a precondition for the economic success of a country.

The traditional Anglo-American concept of the "Rule of Law" is generally defined as consisting of two components: 1) a citizen's obligation to obey the law (the law and order element), and 2) the government's obligation to obey the law (the limited government element). The law and order element, which is the favorite of authoritarian regimes, implies that a government's primary function is to maintain order. The second, which authoritarian regimes ignore, states that the law itself is supreme, not any governmental entity.

English philosopher and physician John Locke, who was an inspiration to our Founders, further tells us that established laws are "not to be varied in particular Cases, but to have one Rule for Rich and Poor, for the Favorite at Court, and the Country Man at Plough." In short the law must apply equally to all men. This is the real meaning of "Due Process" that will be discussed in a later chapter. Strange that our own US Congress is not subject to Social Security that they foisted on the rest of us.

The American version of the "Rule of Law" is probably most famously stated by the noted Harvard law professor Lon Fuller: "the law should consist of general rules that are publicly promulgated, not retroactive, understandable, not contradictory, possible to comply with, stable, and administered as stated."

Fuller also states that if a legal system is missing any of these points it will lead to the failure of the legal system itself. So lets take a closer look at each of his points.

• The lack of rules or laws would lead to anarchy or rule by tyrants. The US is not lacking in an abundance of laws.

• Failure to publicize or make known the rules of law makes it impossible to obey them. While our laws are certainly published and mostly available on the internet, the US Code is in 35 volumes of around 1,200 to 1,400 pages each. This includes 6,850 pages of index in 6 volumes and one volume that is nothing but a 1,400-page list of the other public laws that have not been codified. The Federal Regulations take up an additional 165,000 pages and the Tax Code approximately 67,000 pages. What percentage of these rules and laws do you think you know and understand?

• Retroactive legislation is banned in criminal cases, but our Congress still retroactively changed the penalties for domestic violence laws a few years ago. They have also been known to retroactively change the Tax Code which they claim is legal despite the Bill of Rights' ban on ex post facto laws.

• Legislation that is impossible to understand is epitomized by Obama Care and Speaker of the House Nancy Pelosi's 2010 statement that we have to "pass it to find out what is in it." It contains 2,600 pages of legalese and creates a slew of new government agencies that did nothing but write rules to regulate every aspect of health care and that were still not completed two years after the bill was passed.

• Contradictions in the law make it impossible to comply with, but with only around a quarter million pages of Federal laws and regulations it's hard to believe our leaders would not have been sure to double check that there were no contradictions.

• Demands that are beyond the power of the people would be impossible to comply with.

• Unstable legislation that is subject to frequent revisions makes it impossible to plan for the future and is thus a major drag on the economy and the legal system. Think Obama Care and three years of arguing in Congress over tax rates just for starters.

• Administration of the law must be uniform if it is to have any meaning, but our Courts routinely write their own versions of the law as their mood or political correctness suits them.

If Fuller is right, then our version of the "RULE OF LAW" is in major danger of failure. And those 165,000 pages of rules mentioned above are all written in violation of the Constitution which requires a law to be passed by both houses of Congress and signed by the President before it becomes law. If Congress can't break that rule themselves then how can they give the Executive branch the power to break that rule?

The First Bush v Gore Ruling

Because of the unique circumstances and extraordinary importance of the present case, wherein the Florida Attorney General and the Florida Secretary of State have issued conflicting advisory opinions concerning the propriety of conducting manual recounts, and because of our reluctance to rewrite the Florida Election Code, we conclude that we must invoke the equitable powers of this Court to fashion a remedy that will allow a fair and expeditious resolution of the questions presented here."

With that bit of doublespeak the Florida Supreme Court proceeded to change Florida Law and rule that Must means May, May means Must, and Nov. 14th actually means Nov. 26th . The ruling was immediately appealed to the Supreme Court which granted a very rare expedited hearing.

When Justice Kennedy of the US Supreme Court asked Al Gore's lawyer, "Suppose that after the Nov. 7th election, Florida's Legislature had made by Statute the changes – new deadlines for recounting and certifying votes, selective recounts, and so on – that Florida's Supreme Court made by fiat. Would that have violated the Federal Law that requires presidential elections to be conducted under the rules in place prior to election day?" After first saying that he had never even thought of it, attorney Boles admitted it would be a violation of Federal law because that "would be a legislative enactment as opposed to a judicial interpretation of an existing law." But then he said that what the Florida Supreme Court did was "within the normal ambit of judicial interpretation."

To me these words represent the most stinging indictment of what our judicial system has become that I have ever heard. Our founding fathers sought to create a nation based on the "Rule of Law." But when our nation's top lawyers routinely accept the fact that the law is actually whatever they can talk an activist judge into saying it is, then we no longer live under the "Rule of Law." When a state Supreme Court can unanimously change the law and call it interpretation, then we no longer live under the "Rule of Law." Adherence to the letter of the law and a trust in the Bill of Rights can no longer be considered as absolutes. Only the next judge to rule knows what the law really means.

Think about it. This is one of our nation's top lawyers representing the Vice President of the United States and it never even occurred to him or his team of lawyers that what they had asked the court to do might be considered a change in the law. The question took him totally by surprise. Changing the law by judicial decree is so commonplace today that no one on the Vice President's team even considered the possibility that it might be questioned. It was within the "normal ambit of judicial interpretation". And as long as this pernicious concept holds sway over our nation's law schools and judges we no longer live under the "Rule of Law."

And the decision of the Florida Supreme Court was a unanimous decision. Not one Judge on the court had the integrity to publicly question what the Court was doing. This was the Supreme Court of one of our 50 states. Supposedly the best legal minds that the governor could find. And still they could unanimously change the law and call it judicial interpretation. And so the whims of judges have replaced the "Rule of Law."

It is amazing to me that the United States Supreme Court could actually reach a unanimous decision stating that the actions of the Florida Supreme Court were a violation of Federal law and constituted changing the law after the election had taken place. Even the extremist left wing liberal faction of the Court agreed that the Florida Court had exceeded its authority and changed the law. The example was so extreme that even the radical left could find no politically correct excuse to defend it.

The Court sent the decision back to the Florida Supreme Court with instruction to correct their errors. Instead they only made it worse. This led to the infamous Bush v. Gore case where the US Supreme Court ended the 2000 presidential election and declared Bush the winner by a 5 to 4 vote. However, that decision was in turn based on the forgotten 7 to 2 decision the court based on one of its favorite fraudulent doctrines, "Substantive Equal Protection." The ruling has been reviled by the left ever since. The Court already had a unanimous and just ruling that would have covered this decision, but instead they chose to end the election by doing essentially the same thing that they had just unanimously called unconstitutional when the Florida Supreme Court did it.

How then did we reach the situation we are in today? A situation where courts so routinely legislate from the bench that our vice president can ask the Florida Supreme Court to change the election laws and not one judge on that court sees anything wrong with the request. It is the goal of this book to answer that question.

CHAPTER 3 - ORIGINALISM VS THE "LIVING CONSTITUTION" FRAUD

Justice Hugo Black, U.S. Supreme Court justice and former KKK member said, "When I came on the Supreme Court I never dreamed that we would be making laws."

The very existence of the Constitution of the United States of America is proof that our founding fathers intended that we be a nation based on the "Rule of Law." The Amendment process put forward in that Constitution, both by its existence and the difficulty of the process, is proof that this document was only to be changed by that Amendment process and not by the whims of an Imperial Judiciary. The establishment of the legislature by that Constitution and the powers vested in the legislature by that Constitution provide absolute proof that only the legislature, not the courts, was empowered to write and change the laws.

This statement seems so intuitively obvious that I personally have difficulty understanding how anyone could look at the same set of facts and reach a different conclusion. When I was in school, back in the 60's, I was taught that we had a government based on a separation of powers. That the legislature wrote the laws, the president enforced the laws, and the judges interpreted the laws. And if this led to a politically incorrect judicial opinion it was the responsibility of the legislature, not the court, to fix the law. This was taught as an absolute that we never dreamed of questioning. It was a simple formula that our Founding Fathers used to prevent any branch of government becoming too powerful or tyrannical. Simple, practical, and, in the opinion of many law schools, lawyers, and judges, out of date and old fashioned.

In the Federalist Papers, No. 78 Alexander Hamilton stated that "the judiciary, from the nature of its functions, will always be the least dangerous to the political rights of the constitution; because it will be least in a capacity to annoy or injure them…. It may truly be said to have neither Force nor Will, but merely judgment; and must ultimately depend upon the aid of the executive arm even for the efficacy of its judgments."

Obviously Hamilton felt that a branch of government which has as its only power "Judgment" was not a threat to the rights enumerated in the "constitution". It has no "Force". Whatever the judiciary may rule, they must depend entirely on the executive to enforce those rulings. It has no "Will". It can't decide what the law should be, it can only rule on the law that has been written by the legislature using it's only power "Judgment."

But if the Judiciary is in fact the least dangerous branch of government, how is it that it has become the biggest threat to our Constitutional rights since the Civil War? Hamilton provides us with the answer in the very next paragraph of his argument for lifetime judicial tenure.

"It equally proves, that though individual oppression may now and then proceed from the courts of justice, the general liberty of the people can never be endangered from that quarter: I mean, so long as the judiciary remains truly distinct from both the legislative and executive. For I agree that 'there is no liberty, if the power of judging be not separated from the legislative and executive powers.'"

This is a very powerful statement. "There is no liberty if the power of judging be not separated from the legislative … powers." Even at the very beginning Hamilton could see the danger of allowing judges to legislate from the bench. If judges can legislate then they are, in effect, replacing impartial judgment with their own political agenda. And there is no place for a political agenda on the bench. Our founding fathers created an impartial judiciary, with lifetime tenure, specifically to protect our republican form of government from the political whims of the times. If judges can legislate then that protection evaporates into thin air, and we are at the mercy of whatever "politically correct" fad is popular at the time. Hamilton saw this very clearly and we desperately need to see it also.

In essence the Constitution is a contract between "We the People" and the government. It is just common sense that you can't change the terms of a contract without the consent of the parties involved. Originalism recognizes that contract and believes that it is the duty of the Judge to determine, as best he can, what that contract actually meant when the contracting parties signed it.

Supreme Court Justice Antonin Scalia tells us "I am a textualist. I am an originalist…. My Constitution is not living, it is dead…. Whatever they understood then is, in my view, the meaning … and it's not up to me to say it really shouldn't mean that any more, it should mean something different. Once you get into that boat, you have no criterion."

He continues, "If you somehow adopt a philosophy that the Constitution itself is not static, but rather, it morphs from age to age to say whatever it ought to say — which is probably whatever the people would want it to say — you've eliminated the whole purpose of a constitution. And that's essentially what the 'living constitution' leaves you with."

But my favorite Scalia quote is, "In the old days, they distorted the Constitution in the good old-fashioned way — they lied about it."

We will address several versions of Originalism, Original Intent, Textualism, and Original Understanding, in the next Chapter.

In direct opposition to the honest Interpretation of the law is the fraudulent doctrine of a "Living Constitution" which claims that the Constitution is a living changing document that must adapt itself to modern times and that judges can do the adapting based on their own personal ideas of political correctness. Of course proponents of a "Living Constitution", or at least most of them, would never explain it quite that way themselves.

"Living Constitution" is a term used to describe the Constitution's ability to change to meet the needs of each generation. It is based on the notion that the Constitution of the United States has relevant meaning beyond the original text and is an evolving and dynamic document that changes over time. Therefore the views of today's society should be taken into account when interpreting it.

There are several underlying excuses for the "Living Constitution" theory. The "pragmatist" view contends that interpreting the Constitution in accordance with long outdated views is often unacceptable as a policy matter. According to the pragmatist view a living constitution is a matter of social necessity. When the Constitution was written the original intent was largely to permit many practices universally condemned today. Under this view constitutional requirements of "equal rights" should be read with regard to current standards of equality, and not those of decades or centuries ago, because the alternative would be unacceptable.

The liberal view is that the framers specifically wrote the Constitution in broad and flexible terms to create living document. The living constitution's proponents often cite Edmund Randolph's statement during the writing of the constitution, "two things deserve attention: to insert essential principles only; lest the operations of government should be clogged by rendering those provisions permanent and unalterable, which ought to be accommodated to times and events: and to use simple and precise language, and general propositions." Among other quotes cited in support of the "Living Constitution" is Chief Justice John Marshall's in McCulloch v. Maryland, in which he described the Constitution as "intended to endure for ages to come, and, consequently, to be adapted to the various crises of human affairs."

Here are a few of the arguments offered in support of the "Living Constitution":

1. The original understanding of the Constitution is often

impossible to discover because of the way it was written and ratified. This is just another way of saying it is easier just to make something up than to actually read what the Constitution says.

2. Strict adherence to the original understanding would require overturning vast numbers of precedents, including legal doctrines that are now part of the moral and legal fabric of the nation. In other words it would require correcting the existing liberal frauds that the liberal Court has written into law in disregard of the doctrines that had been part of the legal fabric before they invented the changes.

3. The original understanding may be impossible to translate into modern law in light of the dramatic changes in social conditions. Here they are saying they don't like the original understanding because it might not produce a politically correct result.

4. It allows important changes to occur through the process of interpreting the Constitution and thus minimizes the need to resort to the impossibly difficult amendment process. This is double speak for the American People would never approve the changes they want to make to the Constitution so they have to invent them in the Courts.

5. It encourages judges to admit the influence of their policy views on their legal decisions. Bet you can't find a written decision where they admit it is based on political correctness.

6. It better fits the ability of judges to rely on legal precedent than Originalism which emphasizes historical analysis. Apparently this means that the Law Schools forgot to teach history.

7. It provides a better reason for recognizing the authority of the Constitution, as it has been revised, than Originalism which invokes the authority of long dead lawmakers. Excuse me, but the Constitution was a contract with "We The People", not the lawmakers.

8. And it can justify important Constitutional precedents such as those protecting freedom of expression and condemning segregation which Originalism can't. Give me a break. It was the "Living Constitution" side of our current court that said it was OK for Congress to ration political speech within 60 days of an election in McCain Feingold campaign finance reform. And we will address their false claim that Originalism would have allowed segregation to continue in Brown v. Board of Education in chapter 13.

Perhaps the best argument against the "Living Constitution" is the simple fact that people change. Only the all-knowing elitist left would be arrogant enough to believe that their superior view of political correctness would last until the end of time. In the twenties they adored Fascism,

Socialism, and Communism, but within ten years these progressive movements had been redefined as extreme far right nightmares. A "Living Constitution" can move in both directions. Where a moderate Court just a little to the right of our current Court would return abortion law to the states, as an honest interpretation of the Constitution requires, an extreme right wing Court could use the same fraudulent doctrines as the left to create a ban on abortion out of thin air. Our rights are only truly safe if the Constitution actually means what it says.

"...the risk of assessing evolving standards is that it is all too easy to believe that evolution has culminated in one's own views." – Antonin Scalia

Justice Clarence Thomas stated that there are only two approaches to being a judge: "To try to see as best we can the framers' intentions.", or "Make it up."

CHAPTER 4 - DECONSTRUCTING STRICT CONSTRUCTION

While the term "Strict Construction" is often used to describe mainstream conservative judicial theory, it is actually much maligned in legal circles for being too rigid in its requirement that every word in a law and/or Constitution be taken literally with no deviation allowed.

What comes into play is the "doctrine of absurdity" also called "Scrivener's errors" when strictly following the law produces totally unintended results. An example would be some of the outrageous results stemming from unwavering adherence to zero tolerance policies applied in some schools.

For instance, after Taylor Hess's grandmother had a stroke and was moved to a nursing home, the 16-year-old varsity swim team star loaded some of her things into his pickup and took them to Goodwill. Unfortunately a 10 inch bread knife had fallen into the bed of his pickup. When officials at his high school in Hurst Texas noticed the knife, Hess was expelled for a year.

A related error would be "The Rule of PC Absurdity" or "Erwin's Errors" (which I just invented). "Only obvious injustice is a valid basis for determining Absurdity, never Political Correctness. Any attempt to apply Political Correctness to the Rule of Law will invariably lead to an absurdity which the writers won't even notice."

Judge Roy Moore placed a Ten Commandments monument in his Alabama Courthouse. When a federal judge ordered it removed he appealed GLASSROTH vs. MOORE to the Eleventh Court of Appeals. One of his arguments was that his monument was not a "Law" and that it was only laws which are prohibited by the First Amendment.

The Court treated Moore's argument as absurd and mocked it before citing other precedents for its decision. "The breadth of the Chief Justice's position is illustrated by his counsel's concession at oral argument that if we adopted his position, the Chief Justice would be free to adorn the walls of the Alabama Supreme Court's courtroom with sectarian religious murals and have decidedly religious quotations painted above the bench. Every government building could be topped with a cross, or a menorah, or a statue of Buddha, depending upon the views of the officials with authority over the premises. A crèche could occupy the place of honor in the lobby or rotunda of every municipal, county, state, and federal building. Proselytizing religious messages could be played over the public address system in every government building at the whim of the official in charge of the premises."

The politically correct absurdity is that these justices, by mocking constitutional behaviors, many of which were practiced by the Founders themselves and considered normal for over 180 years, make it impossible to even consider the possibility that Judge Moore could be right. Their view of political correctness blinds them to the idea that the Founders actually meant what they wrote. And yet the Founders put the ten commandments in the Supreme Court building, Jefferson and his Congress went to church in the building where Congress met, Massachusetts collected taxes to support religion until 1833, and virtually all government meetings began with a prayer for over 100 years. While the more extreme behaviors listed may be constitutional there is little likelihood that they would ever be practiced by politicians who wanted to keep their jobs. And of course, the Judges are unable to see that their declaration of absurdity is in fact the true absurdity which makes it an "Erwin's Error." We will address the Supreme Court frauds on this issue in the chapters on the First Amendment.

In the place of Strict Construction modern proponents of basing the interpretation of the law on what it was actually intended to mean call themselves Originalists. There are several views of Originalism that tend to overlap, but all are based on the rather common sense idea that a law and/or Constitution should mean essentially the same thing today as it did when it was written. The differences tend to run together and are often defined differently by different writers.

"Original Intent" attempts to discover what the individuals who wrote a law and/or Constitution actually intended for their words to mean. In the case of the Constitution judges might attempt to deduce the original intent by examining the direct evidence which would be what the writers said during the Constitutional Convention. And they might use indirect evidence which could include what was said during the ratification debates or the meaning of words in common usage or contemporaneous dictionaries.

"Original Understanding" refers to the opinion of the 1648 state convention delegates who ratified the Constitution. This might be found in the records of the ratifying debates, what the Founders said about the law, or the meaning of the words in common usage or dictionaries and legal sources written at that time. With laws which were not ratified it would tend to be a combination of Original Intent and Original Meaning.

"Original Meaning" attempts to discover how the text would have been understood by a reasonable person in the historical period during which the law/Constitution was written. Evidence of original meaning would include the meaning of the words in common usage or dictionaries and legal sources written from that time. Secondary evidence could come from drafting and ratifying conventions and public debates. Phrases such as "due process" and "freedom of the press" had well established meanings long before the Constitution was written.

Judge Bork in his book "The Tempting of America" describes "Original Understanding" as follows; "It is the meaning understood at the time of the law's enactment. Though I have written of the understanding of the ratifiers of the Constitution, since they enacted it and made it law, that is actually a shorthand formulation, because what the ratifiers understood themselves to be enacting must be taken to be what the public of that time would have understood the words to mean." In short Bork uses one current definition of "Original Meaning" as his definition of "Original Understanding."

In practice all versions of Originalism will generally reach the same or at least a similar conclusion. And the Originalist will tend to use whatever mix produces the clearest understanding of what the law meant at the time it was enacted.

Justice Antonin Scalia tells us that he is a Textualist first and an Originalist second. Scalia has said, "A text should not be construed strictly, and it should not be construed leniently; it should be construed reasonably, to contain all that it fairly means."

When representatives write a law and/or Constitution they have a general tendency to actually say what they mean. In the case of the Constitution these were men who were from a time in history where they were much more rigorously trained in English grammar than anyone but an English major in college would be today. It therefore makes total sense to assume that they chose their words carefully and, after much debate and compromise, chose words that said what they intended them to say.

Textualism is an approach to the interpretation which says that a statute's ordinary meaning should govern its interpretation, rather than inquiring into the purpose of those who wrote the text. Under this view the legislative history of a statute should not be allowed to trump the text itself. The Textualist will examine the structure of the law and hear the words as they would sound to an objective reasonable person living at the time the law was written.

Textualist judges have argued that courts should not treat committee reports or sponsor's statements as accurate evidence of legislative intent. After all a 535 member legislature probably has no collective intent concerning the meaning of a law and, even if they did, there would be no reliable way to know if the views of a committee or sponsor were the same as the intent of Congress as a whole. It is the law that governs, not the intent of the lawgiver. And it should be the original meaning of the law that governs and not it's evolving meaning over time.

The basic steps followed by the Textualist would be to:

1. Look at the plain meaning of the words of the Constitution/law as they were understood at the time they were written. This would primarily involve looking at contemporaneous dictionaries and grammar books.

2. If the original meaning of the words is still hard to understand then the Textualist would look for public statements for the time when the Constitution/law was written. This might help understand what it meant to those who actually ratified it into law.

3. If it is still remains unclear then they could turn to any private statements about the text that were written before or at the time the Constitution/law was ratified. These should be used only if they clarify the public meaning of the law.

4. Least reliable would be the history of how the law was viewed or applied after it was ratified. This should only be used if it helps understand what the text meant to those who ratified it.

To the extent that Textualism uses Originalism to clarify the meaning when the words are ambiguous it reduces the possibility of Scrivener's Errors. That is as long as Originalism is used to interpret the meaning of an ambiguous text rather than override the meaning of a clear one.

CHAPTER 5. – STARE DECISIS OR NEVER FIX A LIBERAL JUDICIAL ERROR

An important doctrine of law is known as "Stare Decisis" or "to stand by that which is decided."

As mentioned in an earlier chapter John Adams tells us that, "No man will contend that a nation can be free that is not governed by fixed laws. All other government than that of permanent known laws is the government of mere will and pleasure."

"Stare Decisis" is based on the assumption that certainty, predictability, and stability in the law are important objectives of the legal system. However, historically it has always been considered as an important guideline rather than a fixed rule. It is only recently that the left has tried to maintain that it is an unbreakable rule, especially with regard to "legislation" that has been passed by the left wing of the Court.

The left asserts that all precedents are presumed to be well-founded, unbiased legal decisions, rather than political decisions, and that they not only have the authority of the original constitutional decisions, but that each additional layer of precedents actually becomes even more authoritative than the Constitution or the law on which it is based. They add further that the longer a precedent has been in effect and the more it is embedded or entrenched in society the more disruptive it would be if it was overturned.

And, to make matters even worse, it has become the custom of lower courts and the press to treat the entire decision, including the explanation of the decision, as law, even though it is only the Court Order itself that is supposed to have the force of law.

In July 2009, Senator Spector even tried to get perspective Justice Sonia Sotomayor to agree that Roe v. Wade was a super precedent that could not be overturned. Her refusal is perhaps the only thing she has ever said that I agree with.

Our first Chief Justice John Marshall in Marbury v. Madison tells us that, "Certainly all those who have framed written Constitutions contemplate them as forming the fundamental and paramount law of the nation, and consequently the theory of every such government must be that an act of the Legislature repugnant to the Constitution is void."

It would seem obvious that no amount of excuse making can change something that is void into a law that is legitimate.

Marshall continues, "it is apparent that the framers of the Constitution contemplated that instrument as a rule for the government of courts, as well as of the Legislature."

If the Court is bound by the Constitution then there is no way that they can legitimately claim that a law which is void is not. This is especially true if the law was unconstitutionally written by the Court itself (Courts have no authority under the constitution to legislate).

In 1983 in Smith v. Allwright, Justices White , O'Connor, and Rehnquist wrote "Although we must be mindful of the 'desirability of continuity of decision in constitutional questions, … when convinced of former error, this Court has never felt constrained to follow precedent. In constitutional questions, when correction depends on amendment and not upon legislative action this Court throughout its history has freely exercised its power to reexamine the basis of its constitutional decisions.'"

Justice Douglas agrees that "A judge looking at a constitutional decision may have compulsions to revere past history and accept what was once written. But he remembers above all else that it is the Constitution which he swore to support and defend, not the gloss his predecessors may have put on it."

Bouvier's Law Dictionary from 1856 provides historical support for essentially the same interpretation of the doctrine.

"Stare decisis. To abide or adhere to decided cases.

2. It is a general maxim that when a point has been settled by decision, it forms a precedent which is not afterwards to be departed from. The doctrine of stare decisis is not always to be relied upon, for the courts find it necessary to overrule cases which have been hastily decided, or contrary to principle. Many hundreds of such overruled cases may be found in the American and English books of reports."

And history actually shows that on average the Court overturns one or two prior decisions every year. In his essay "Overruled: Stare Decisis in the US Supreme Court" Ronald B. Standler has documented 74 opinions that were overturned in the 46 years from 1960 to 2005.

Judge Bork tells us that "The Supreme Court frequently overrules its own precedent…. The New Deal Court swiftly began overruling or ignoring precedent, some of it of fifty years' standing, and often did so by five-to-four votes.... Swift v. Taylor held in 1842 that federal courts could apply a "general Law" independent of the state law that would apply had the suit been brought in a state court sitting nearby. The rule lasted ninety-six years. Erie Railroad Co. v. Tompkins did away with it in 1938. Plessy v. Ferguson and the rule of separate-but-equal in racial matters, lasted fifty-eight years before it was dispatched in Brown v. Board of Education."

If they were actually being honest about it, one of the biggest reasons Judges may invoke Stare Decisis and past precedents to keep the law the same is to avoid the embarrassment of admitting that they made a mistake. It is better in their eyes for the Court to Save Face and preserve its integrity than to be true to the law or the Constitution. I hold that a Court that subverts the Constitution has no integrity to protect.

The other overriding reason seems to be to provide legitimacy for questionable decisions. To this degree at least the liberal wing of the court is "Highly Qualified", at least to write reasonable sounding excuses for laws and the Constitution not meaning what they actually say.

And so the blatant hypocrisy of the left brings us full circle from the Living Constitution to Stare Decisis and back again. We must have a Living Constitution so that it can be changed on any politically correct whim as long as the winds of change are blowing from the left. However, as soon as the moderate Justices want to revisit the Constitution, we are supposed to apply an immovable Stare Decisis on steroids that I call Erwin's Error #2 or the "Frozen Constitution Doctrine."

Of course it makes complete sense to the all-wise elites on the left who know in their hearts that they are much smarter than "We the People". What they will never understand is that 350,000,000 people making dozens of decisions a day in their own enlightened self-interest represent millions of times more combined wisdom than the elites will ever have in their wildest dreams.

CHAPTER 6. MARBURY V. MADISON OR MARSHALL CREATES THE IMPERIAL JUDICIARY

1803 became one of the turning points in Judicial History with the case of Marbury v. Madison. With this case Chief Justice John Marshall established the principles of supremacy of the Constitution, the subordination of the three branches of government to the Constitution, and Judicial Review which gave the Court the ability to declare a law unconstitutional.

Those advocating the expansion of federal power, to which Marshall most certainly belonged, claim that this case declared that the Courts were superior to the other branches of the government and established supremacy of the judiciary. Although we seem to casually accept that as the case today it is not necessarily true as we shall see.

The details of the case are technically confusing and not very relevant to the end result. The case resulted from a petition to the Supreme Court by William Marbury, who was appointed by President John Adams to be Justice of the Peace in the District of Columbia but whose commission was never delivered. Marbury asked the Supreme Court to force the new Secretary of State James Madison to deliver the commission.

It is interesting to note that in order to produce the results he wanted Marshall had to literally change the Constitution by misquoting it. Article II section 2. of the US Constitution reads "In all Cases affecting Ambassadors, other public Ministers and Consuls, and those in which a State shall be Party, the supreme Court shall have original Jurisdiction. In all the other Cases before mentioned, the supreme Court shall have appellate Jurisdiction, both as to Law and Fact, with such Exceptions, and under such Regulations as the Congress shall make."

Marshall quoted the above passage as follows: "the supreme court shall have original jurisdiction, in all cases affecting ambassadors, other public ministers and consuls, and those in which a state shall be a party. In all other cases, the supreme court shall have appellate jurisdiction." With much legalese these changes reversed jurisdiction from the appellate court to the Supreme Court which actually had no authority to hear the case. And it allowed Marshall to rule against Marbury on the grounds that the Judiciary Act of 1789 that enabled Marbury to bring his claim to the Supreme Court was itself unconstitutional. That said, it was the commentary on the decision that made this case historic.

The most pertinent and famous words from the decision are self-explanatory, "Certainly all those who have framed written constitutions contemplate them as forming the fundamental and paramount law of the nation, and consequently the theory of every such government must be, that an act of the legislature repugnant to the constitution is void."

Marshall further states that," This theory is essentially attached to a written constitution, and is consequently to be considered by this court as one of the fundamental principles of our society."

Marshall eloquently justifies the principle of Judicial Review saying, "It is emphatically the province and duty of the judicial department to say what the law is. Those who apply the rule to particular cases, must of necessity expound and interpret that rule. If two laws conflict with each other, the courts must decide on the operation of each. So if a law be in opposition to the constitution: if both the law and the constitution apply to a particular case, so that the court must either decide that case conformably to the law, disregarding the constitution; or conformably to the constitution, disregarding the law: the court must determine which of these conflicting rules governs the case. This is of the very essence of judicial duty…. If then the courts are to regard the constitution; and the constitution is superior to any ordinary act of the legislature; the constitution, and not such ordinary act, must govern the case to which they both apply."

With those words he correctly states that when there is a conflict between the Constitution and the law it is the duty of the Court to resolve that conflict in favor of the Constitution.

But he tempers those words with the admonition that the Courts are also bound by the Constitution, "the particular phraseology of the constitution of the United States confirms and strengthens the principle, supposed to be essential to all written constitutions, that a law repugnant to the constitution is void, and that courts, as well as other departments, are bound by that instrument."

Jefferson hated the decision. "You seem to consider the judges as the ultimate arbiters of all constitutional questions; a very dangerous doctrine indeed, and one which would place us under the despotism of an oligarchy."

Indeed that is what most of us, including many Justices themselves, believe has happened. As Justice Jackson commented on Marbury, "We are not final because we are infallible, but we are infallible only because we are final." Or the remark of Charles Evans Hughes who later became Chief Justice of the United States, "We are under the Constitution, but the Constitution is what the judges say it is…"

In truth there is not a single word in Marbury which says that the Supreme Court has an "exclusive" right to decide the Constitutionality of a law. It only states that, when there is a conflict with the Constitution that is brought before the Court, it is the duty of the Court to make a ruling favoring the Constitution. And there is not a word in the constitution that denies any of the co-equal branches of government, or the governments of the states, the right to declare that a law is "repugnant to the constitution" and thus void. An honest branch of Congress, of which we currently have none, would feel bound by their oaths to honor the Constitution and not pass unconstitutional laws. A president who truly took his oath seriously, which we have not seen in my lifetime, would refuse to implement a law or Court decision that was unconstitutional. And states would refuse to honor and or enforce unconstitutional laws. All of these actions would be politically very difficult, but not impossible.

It was decades later that Andrew Jackson declared, "John Marshall has made his decision; let him enforce it now if he can."

And it was only shortly before Marbury that two states declared the "Alien and Sedition Acts" unconstitutional. These acts unconstitutionally banned the Democratic-Republican party opposing President Adams from criticizing the government. Thomas Jefferson and James Madison, through the Virginia and Kentucky Resolutions of 1798 and 1799, declared that states had the right to actively nullify and resist unconstitutional actions of the federal government. Jefferson warned that, "unless arrested at the threshold," the Alien and Sedition Acts would "necessarily drive these states into revolution and blood." This problem was eventually resolved politically by the election of Jefferson as President.

The influence of Jefferson's doctrine of states' rights is said to have been the theory that led to the Civil War. President James Garfield, at the close of the Civil War, said that Jefferson's Kentucky Resolution "contained the germ of nullification and secession, and we are today reaping the fruits".

Most people believe that this nullification and secession issue was settled by the Civil War, but in truth it is only settled for issues that the federal government is willing to go to war to defend. The only thing that is settled is that none of our governors and state legislatures have the stomach for the constitutional and political crisis it would precipitate. Perhaps it is time for the states to stand again for the rights and freedoms that their contract with the federal government was supposed to guarantee.

CHAPTER 7 - BARON V. BALTIMORE OR WHY THE BILL OF RIGHTS DIDN'T APPLY TO THE STATES - SORT OF MAYBE

The case of Baron v. Baltimore is a landmark decision from 1833 which declared that the Bill of Rights does not apply to the states. Although it is settled law that is unlikely to ever be overturned or even questioned by the legal establishment, it is important because it sets up the conditions for the Court to later fraudulently create new law that applies bits and pieces of the Bill of Rights to the states and to the people in a totally inconsistent and politically correct manner using the doctrine of "Incorporation" that will be discussed in later chapters.

It is also interesting to note that there are numerous reasons to doubt that the decision was accurate despite Chief Justice Marshall's statement that "The question thus presented is, we think, of great importance, but not of much difficulty."

The facts of the case are simple. The city of Baltimore had diverted the flow of streams and in doing so made the water at Baron's wharf in the harbor too shallow to use. He was seeking relief under the takings clause of the Fifth Amendment which would only apply if the Bill of rights affected the states.

Marshall said "The Constitution was ordained and established by the people of the United States for themselves, for their own government, and not for the government of the individual States.... The powers they conferred on this government were to be exercised by itself, and the limitations on power, if expressed in general terms, are naturally, and we think necessarily, applicable to the government created by the instrument."

In truth the Constitution not only created the Federal Government, it also created the Union between the states and their relationship to the federal government. If the provisions of the amendments had been inserted into the original text of the constitution in one of the sections specifying application to the states or Congress, then the above would be true. But Congress chose to make them individual stand-alone amendments. They were also considered for ratification one at a time. Therefore the fact that the First Amendment specifies application to Congress only, implies that the others do not have this same limitation. This application to Congress only was undoubtedly based on the impossibility of passing the First Amendment if it banned the establishments that existed in the majority of states at that time. (See the chapter on the Establishment Clause).

Marshall also said "In their several Constitutions, they have imposed such restrictions on their respective governments, as their own wisdom suggested, such as they deemed most proper for themselves. It is a subject on which they judge exclusively, and with which others interfere no further than they are supposed to have a common interest." But in article one section 10 they did impose restrictions on the states.

Marshall added "If the original Constitution, in the ninth and tenth sections of the first article, draws this plain and marked line of discrimination between the limitations it imposes on the powers of the General Government and on those of the State; if, in every inhibition intended to act on State power, words are employed which directly express that intent; some strong reason must be assigned for departing from this safe and judicious course in framing the amendments before that departure can be assumed. We search in vain for that reason."

And since when did any legislature have to have a good reason for anything it did. However, selling the Bill of Rights to the people was quite possibly that reason. A major campaign was mounted praising it as a BILL OF RIGHTS, and in those days rights were considered to belong to the people and not to the state. If the states ratified rights and those rights belonged to the people, then those states were in effect recognizing the existence of those rights.

Marshall also said the states could have amended their own constitutions. "Had the people of the several States, or any of them, required changes in their Constitutions, had they required additional safeguards to liberty from the apprehended encroachments of their particular governments, the remedy was in their own hands, and could have been applied by themselves." However, why would there be any need if the states felt that the US Constitution had already covered the issue?

Marshall finished saying "These amendments contain no expression indicating an intention to apply them to the State governments. This court cannot so apply them."

In fact that is my trump card. Madison's version of the Second Amendment reads, "The right of the people to keep and bear arms shall not be infringed; a well armed, and well regulated militia being the best security of a free country; but no person religiously scrupulous of bearing arms, shall be compelled to render military service in person." There was no federal militia, so the Amendment could not have provided an exemption from military service if it did not apply to the states.

And the Congressional debates clearly indicate that this exemption would in fact have applied to the militia.

The Congressional Register, 17 August 1789: "Mr. Benson — Moved to have the words "But no person religiously scrupulous shall be compelled to bear arms" struck out. He would always leave it to the benevolence of the legislature — for, modify it, said he, as you please, it will be impossible to express it in such a manner as to clear it from ambiguity. No man can claim this indulgence of right. It may be a religious persuasion, but it is no natural right, and therefore ought to be left to the discretion of the government. If this stands part of the constitution, it will be a question before the judiciary, on every regulation you make with respect to the organization of the militia, whether it comports with this declaration or not? It is extremely injudicious to intermix matters of doubt with fundamentals."

The Second Amendment was clearly to have applied to the states in the minds of the House of Representatives that passed it, so there can be little doubt in my mind that Baron v. Baltimore was decided wrong.

And Marshall also had a political reason for his finding. If the Fifth Amendment applied to the states then slaves could claim that they had been deprived of liberty without due process. In 1833 that would have certainly sparked the Civil War years earlier.

Nevertheless, this decision is one which has become so much a part of the law that it will never be revisited by the Court.

CHAPTER 8 – DRED SCOTT V. SANFORD OR HOW TO CREATE RIGHTS OUT OF THIN AIR

"And the notion that the Due Process Clause of the Fifth Amendment is a wellspring of unenumerated rights against the Federal Government 'strains credulity for even the most casual user of words.'" - Justice Thomas in McDonald v. Chicago

It was 54 years before the high court again overturned a law enacted by Congress. But in 1857 Dred Scott v. Sanford created new law, helped elect Lincoln, inflamed the country to war, and entered history as the worst decision ever devised by the US Supreme Court.

Again the facts of the case are fairly simple. Dred Scott was a slave who was taken by his master from the slave state of Missouri to the free state of Illinois and then to the free territory of Wisconsin. When his master returned to Missouri, he took Scott with him back to that slave state. In 1846, Scott was helped to sue for his freedom in court by Abolitionist lawyers who claimed he should be free since he had lived on free soil. The case went all the way to the United States Supreme Court. Chief Justice Roger B. Taney, with encouragement from President Buchannan, decided to make the question of slavery "Settled Law".

In 1857 seven out of nine Justices on the Supreme Court declared no slave or descendant of a slave could be a U.S. citizen, or ever had been a U.S. citizen. Since he was not a citizen Scott had no rights and could not sue in a Federal Court and therefore must remain a slave.

The Supreme Court also ruled that Congress could not stop slavery in the territories and declared the Missouri Compromise of 1820 to be unconstitutional. The Missouri Compromise prohibited slavery north of the parallel 36°30´ in the Louisiana Purchase. The Court ruled that the law violated the Fifth Amendment of the Constitution which prohibits Congress from depriving persons of their property without due process of law. In effect they declared all of the free states and territories slave states and territories.

It seemed that the Missouri Compromise, which had stood for thirty-seven years, was unconstitutional. Congress could not restrict slavery anywhere because by doing so, Congress would deny slaveholders "due process of law." And by removing slavery from the democratic process they made any peaceful solution to the problem of slavery impossible.

They even invoked Erwin's Error #2, the Rule of Judicial Absurdity, which states that any attempt to apply Political Correctness to the Rule of Law will invariably lead to a Scrivener's Error which the writers won't even notice. Thus the Court stated that if they ruled in favor of Scott "It would give to persons of the negro race, ...the right to enter every other State whenever they pleased, ...to sojourn there as long as they pleased, to go where they pleased ...the full liberty of speech in public and in private upon all subjects upon which its own citizens might speak; to hold public meetings upon political affairs, and to keep and carry arms wherever they went."

And thus we have the first use of the "Substantive Due Process" fraud by the US Supreme Court.

The Fifth Amendment reads in part "No person shall be held to answer for a capital, or otherwise infamous crime, unless on a presentment or indictment of a Grand Jury,… nor be deprived of life, liberty, or property, without due process of law; nor shall private property be taken for public use, without just compensation.

In fact "Due Process of Law" means exactly what it says. Whatever processes are written into the law are due to everyone and must be applied equally in all cases. When a government harms a person without following the law exactly, it is a violation of "Due Process". To send a person to trial for a capital crime without the indictment of a Grand Jury would be a violation of "Due Process."

It finds its roots in British law. In clause 39 of the Magna Carta, John of England promised as follows: "No free man shall be seized or imprisoned, or stripped of his rights or possessions, or outlawed or exiled, or deprived of his standing in any other way, nor will we proceed with force against him, or send others to do so, except by the lawful judgment of his equals or by the law of the land."

Alexander Hamilton, addressing the New York Assembly in 1787, stated that the "words 'due process' have a precise technical meaning, and are only applicable to the process and proceedings of the courts of justice; they can never be referred to an act of the legislature."

In other words it is failure to follow the law that is a violation of "Due Process." A statute, by definition, cannot violate "Due Process." A law can establish the "Due Process" that must be followed, but it cannot violate

"Due Process" itself. And that had long been the universal understanding of the term by 1789 when the Bill of Rights was written and remained so for nearly 70 years after that. But that is exactly what Taney did; declare that a statute violated "Due Process."

The doctrine of "Substantive Due Process" holds that the "Due Process" clause not only protects basic procedural rights, but that it also protects substantive rights which are those general rights that reserve to an individual the power to possess or to do certain things. It attempts to convert "Due Process" into Due Rights with the Supreme Court having sole discretion as to which rights to invent and how to apply them. It would in fact be more accurate to call it the Subjective Process doctrine.

"Substantive Due Process" greatly expands the power of judicial review in several ways:

1. First, it gives the federal courts total discretion to decide what substantive rights are protected under "Due Process" and how that protection is to be applied.

2. Under the "Incorporation" doctrine the Court picks and chooses those politically correct parts of the Bill of Rights it wants to apply to the states and arbitrarily applies each to the states in a different way that meets the Courts predetermined political outcome. (We will discuss Incorporation in later chapters.)

3. Under the "Fundamental Rights" theory the Court invents whatever substantive rights it wants by claiming that they are so fundamental that the Founders must have intended to protect them even though they are not mentioned in the Constitution. Instead the Court claims these guarantees emanate from the word "Liberty" in the Fourteenth Amendment's Due Process Clause or are found in "penumbras" surrounding the other Constitutional Amendments.

4. After the Court invents a substantive right it can then enforce that right on the states by reviewing all state legislation for compliance with it.

Scalia calls the doctrine an "Oxymoron" and suggests that it is "past time for the Court to abandon this Alfred Hitchcock line of our jurisprudence."

Given the ill repute in which the Dred Scott decision was held, it even gave "Substantive Due Process" a bad name for a short a time after that. But the idea of being able to create rights out of thin air would prove too tempting for future Justices, right, left, and even moderate to ignore.

CHAPTER 9. THE COURT TAKES THE 14TH AMENDMENT TO THE SLAUGHTERHOUSE

The Fourteenth Amendment, Section 1, reads in full: "All persons born or naturalized in the United States and subject to the jurisdiction thereof, are citizens of the United States and of the State wherein they reside. No State shall make or enforce any law which shall abridge the privileges or immunities of citizens of the United States; nor shall any State deprive any person of life, liberty, or property, without due process of law; nor deny to any person within its jurisdiction the equal protection of the laws."

Needless to say, a "Due Process" clause that applies to the states would eventually become even more dangerous to the honest interpretation of the Constitution than the clause in the Fifth Amendment that only applies to the Federal Government. The Slaughterhouse cases of 1873 made that even more likely.

The river at New Orleans was polluted by the Slaughterhouses upstream. To correct the problem Louisiana passed a statute that limited the places in which animals could be slaughtered for food to a location south of the city; granted a monopoly to a single private company to manage and operate slaughterhouses; and required butchers to pay a fee to that company to engage in their trade of slaughtering animals. Three of the Lawsuits filed by the butchers were consolidated and made it to the U.S. Supreme Court.

The Butchers claimed that the law was unconstitutional because it imposed "involuntary servitude" on them, and violated the "privileges and immunities," clause and denied "equal protection of the laws," and deprived them of "liberty and property without due process of law."

The Court dismissed their "involuntary servitude" argument saying The Thirteenth Amendment was directed at abolishing slavery, not trade regulations.

On the due process and equal protection arguments brought under the Fourteenth Amendment the Court said, "it is sufficient to say that under no construction of that provision that we have ever seen, or any that we deem admissible, can the restraint imposed by the State of Louisiana upon the exercise of their trade by the butchers of New Orleans be held to be a deprivation of property within the meaning of that provision." And "We doubt very much whether any action of a State not directed by way of discrimination against the negroes as a class, or on account of their race, will ever be held to come within the purview of this provision." I'm not sure exactly what all that means either but historically it has not put any restraint on the "Due Process" clause.

On the "Privileges and Immunities" clause Justice Miller said that the 14th Amendment distinguished between citizenship of a state and citizenship of the United States. He then observed that the amendment expressly applied only to the privileges and immunities arising from citizenship in the United States and did not include private property rights, freedom of contract and freedom from arbitrary government interference with the right to engage in enterprise and extended only to those specified in the U.S. Constitution.

For our purposes it is enough to understand that by effectively nullifying the Privileges and Immunities Clause the Court's ability to project federal power on the states was limited. Judges on the right and left were forced to turn to the "Substantive Due Process" fraud to avoid the precedent of the Slaughterhouse Cases.

Judge Bork agrees saying that "Miller was following a sound judicial instinct: to reject a construction of the new amendment that would leave the Court at large in the field of public policy without any guidelines other than the views of its members."

A Textualist might see it differently. Precedent says the "Privileges and Immunities" clause has essentially no meaning, but if words are always intended to have meaning and the clause referred to basic enumerated rights then it quite logically would apply the Bill of Rights to the states. "No State shall make or enforce any law which shall abridge the privileges or immunities of citizens of the United States."

Justice Thomas agrees with that view and I feel it has merit. In Justice Thomas' concurring opinion in McDonald v. Chicago he argues that it was common usage at the time to use the words Privileges, Immunities, and Rights more or less interchangeably. This definition would allow the Bill of Rights to be applied to the States without resorting to the "Due Process" fraud.

Thomas says "But I cannot agree that it (The Second Amendment) is enforceable against the States through a clause that speaks only to "process." Instead, the right to keep and bear arms is a privilege of

American citizenship that applies to the States through the Fourteenth Amendment's Privileges or Immunities Clause.... In my view, the record makes plain that the Framers of the Privileges or Immunities Clause and the ratifying-era public understood—just as the Framers of the Second Amendment did—that the right to keep and bear arms was essential to the preservation of liberty. The record makes equally plain that they deemed this right necessary to include in the minimum baseline of federal rights that the Privileges or Immunities Clause established in the wake of the War over slavery."

He also warned that the "Privileges or Immunities" clause could potentially be perverted as was the "Due Process" clause. "A separate question is whether the privileges and immunities of American citizenship include any rights besides those enumerated in the Constitution.... Because this case does not involve an unenumerated right, it is not necessary to resolve the question whether the Clause protects such rights, or whether the Court's judgment in Slaughter-House was correct."

At the very least Thomas' opinion would give the court a chance to apply the Bill of Rights to the States in a rational manner instead of the totally unconstitutional hodge-podge of political correctness they based on "Due Process" and called "Incorporation". We will cover this fraud in a later chapter.

CHAPTER 10. – THERE ONCE WAS A REAL RIGHT WING COURT

Between the time of the Civil War and the Great Depression the Court was in fact a right wing court that expanded the doctrine of "Substantive Due Process" to advance causes to the right of the letter of the law and in the process make the doctrine an accepted legal fraud.

Judge Bork tells us that "substantive due process, wherever it appears, is never more than a pretense that the Judge's views are in the Constitution."

In the 1897 case of Allgeyer v. Louisiana the Court for the first time used "Substantive Due Process" to strike down a state statute. Before that time, the Court generally had used the Commerce Clause to invalidate state legislation. The Allgeyer case concerned a Louisiana law that banned contracts with insurance firms in other states. The Court found that the law unfairly abridged the right to enter into lawful contracts, as guaranteed by the "Due Process Clause" of the Fourteenth Amendment. The Court argued that "liberty" in the clause meant "liberty of contract" which the Court would use to strike down state regulation of private industry such as maximum working hours or minimum wages.

The Louisiana legislature had already decided that Allgeyer's out of state purchase of insurance was unlawful. Justice Peckham's decision stated that he and not the legislature would decide what was lawful. To add to the open ended unlawfulness of the Court Peckham added "When and how far (the states legislative) power may be legitimately exercised with regard to these subjects must be left for determination to each case as it arises." Not only had the court invented a new law but it, and only it, could decide when it applied. This was a total fraud on steroids.

For the next 40 years after Allgeyer the Court would use what has been called the freedom-of-contract version of "Substantive Due Process" to invent rights that would help big business. Corporate giants, like the

Rockefellers and the Carnegies, influenced the law to protect their wealth, industry, and position at the expense of the Constitution and the little guy.

Lochner v. New York in 1905 is often considered the symbol of this judicial usurpation of power. The Court struck down a New York law that prohibited employers from allowing workers in bakeries to be on the job more than ten hours per day and 60 hours per week. The Court found that the law was not a valid exercise of the state's Police Power or power to make any legislation not forbidden by the constitution. This time Justice Peckham decided that the power had limits independent of the Constitution, and that judges could enforce those limits even when the Constitution was silent. Judges were now free to decide what was or was not a proper legislative purpose.

In Lochner Justice Peckham asks "Are we all ... at the mercy of legislative majorities?" Judge Bork tells us the answer must be yes. "Being 'at the mercy of legislative majorities' is merely another way of describing the basic American plan: representative democracy. We may all deplore the results from time to time, but that does not empower judges to set them aside: the Constitution allows only voters to do that." That is unless there is a legitimate violation of the Constitution.

CHAPTER 11. - FDR AND THE NULLIFICATION OF THE 10TH AMENDMENT

By the 1930's the use of "Substantive Due Process" to strike down economic regulations passed by the states had become highly unpopular with progressives, not because it was illegitimate (which it was), but because its judge invented rights became politically incorrect.

At the national level the Court blocked federal regulations by finding that they were not within the scope of the enumerated congressional powers in Article 1 section 8 of the Constitution. The court regularly struck down federal regulations as going beyond the government's power to regulate interstate commerce or to lay and collect taxes.

On these points the Court was legitimately protecting the Tenth Amendment which holds that "The powers not delegated to the United States by the Constitution, nor prohibited by it to the States, are reserved to the states respectively, or to the people." However, it infuriated President Roosevelt and his New Deal supporters.

The Courts struck down Roosevelt's National Industrial Recovery Act of 1932 which allowed the president to place wage, hour, and trade restrictions on industry. It also struck down the Railroad Retirement Act of 1934 and the Bituminous Coal Conservation Act of 1935.

The administration feared that the National Labor Relations Act and Social Security Act might also be in danger. Roosevelt attempted to increase the size of the Court so he could pack it with supporters. He failed in that but remained President long enough to appoint a liberal majority to the Court and then significantly increase the size and power of the Federal government by greatly increasing the Congress' power to regulate commerce and taxes.

The Commerce Clause of the Constitution gives Congress the power "To regulate Commerce with foreign Nations, and among the several States, and with the Indian Tribes."

Judge Bork argues that prior to 1887 the Commerce Clause was rarely invoked by Congress, and thus a broad interpretation of the word "commerce" was clearly never intended by the Founders. The word Commerce, as used in the Constitutional Convention and the Federalist Papers, can be substituted with either the word "trade" or "exchange" while preserving the meaning of the statements. It is obvious to Originalists and anyone else with even limited common sense that the word was never intended to mean more than that. The Commerce Clause was only intended to let Congress regulate trade between states.

In 1942 it became a license for Congress to regulate almost everything. In Wickard v. Filburn the Court upheld the Agricultural Adjustment Act of 1938, which sought to stabilize wide fluctuations in the market price for wheat. The Court found that Congress could apply national quotas to wheat grown on a farmer's own land, for his own consumption, because the total of such local production and consumption could potentially be sufficiently large enough to impact the overall national goal of stabilizing prices. The Court also said that "whether the subject of the regulation in question was "production," "consumption," or "marketing" is, therefore, not material for purposes of deciding the question of federal power before us." Commerce equals trade became commerce equals every aspect of production, consumption, and marketing even if it takes place entirely on your own property.

"Substantive Due Process" was no longer used to protect businesses. And in United States v. Caroline Products new ideas for inventing laws and rights were introduced. In this case the Court upheld a federal prohibition of interstate shipment of "Filled Milk" which was milk with any fat or oil other than milk in it. In a footnote on the case Justice Stone struck another blow for Judicial illegitimacy.

He said that "There may be a narrower scope for operation of the presumption of constitutionality when legislation appears on its face to be within a specific prohibition of the Constitution, such as those of the first ten amendments, which are deemed equally specific when held to be embraced within the Fourteenth." The only legitimate operation of presumption in such a case would be that it is unconstitutional, but Justice Stone had a different idea. "…whether prejudice against discrete and insular minorities may be a special condition, which tends seriously to curtail the operation of those political processes ordinarily to be relied upon to protect minorities, and which may call for a correspondingly more searching judicial inquiry." And with that bit of doublespeak, our Constitution which protects religious, national, and racial minorities, now suddenly protects "discrete and insular minorities," defined as any minority the Court can define, from anything the Court decides is prejudice.

Skinner v. Oklahoma made matters even worse. An Oklahoma law said that anyone who had two or more felony convictions involving moral turpitude would be sterilized. Today, when it is called cruel and unusual to deny a prisoner a TV set, they would have called it that, but back then they still recognized that it didn't fit the long standing definition of cruel and unusual. Therefore, since the Judge found the punishment intolerable, he had to find a different excuse for overturning it.

Justice Douglas decided to use the "Equal Protection" clause that an earlier Court said only applied to racial equality. The law treated embezzlement (white collar) convictions different than larceny convictions. And since this was a case that involved "one of the basic civil rights of man" the "Equal Protection" clause could be applied.

There is of course nothing in the Constitution that makes fertility a right, but Douglas had invented "Substantive Equal Protection" so it didn't matter. Judges could now use equality to invent law as long as it involved a "basic civil right". This is an obvious fraud because if everything must be equal it would be impossible. The rich should have equal tax rates. I should have an equal pension and medical plan with members of Congress. And while I consider the right to keep and bear arms a "basic civil right" it took the Court over 200 years to admit it.

The Court now had so many ways to make up laws and rights that it was easy to achieve politically correct results using legal arguments and precedents that actually sounded legitimate. The Warren Court would soon make good use of them all.

CHAPTER 12. – THE WARREN COURT OR IF WE LIKE IT WE WILL CALL IT CONSTITUTIONAL

By 1953, and the time of the Warren Court, the Yale Law School was teaching the doctrine of Arrested Legal Realism. Basically put, a judge chooses his results and then reasons backwards to find a legal excuse for it. At this point in time there were so many fraudulent doctrines and unconstitutional precedents to choose from that any result desired could be justified using reasoning that sounds legitimate and any honest judge would admit that this is how he decides cases. This doctrine gave the dishonest judge the solace of believing it was OK because everyone else was doing it. A statement that was only too true of the majority on the Warren Court.

They made so much bad law that it will suffice to list a few rather than bore you by trying to explain it all. However, some of the cases will be addressed in more detail when we address specific frauds in later chapters.

Brown v. Board of Education (1954) banned the segregation of public schools based on the Equal Protection Clause. It was a good decision that was poorly written and caused much misunderstanding as we shall see in the next chapter.

The one man, one vote cases, Baker v. Carr and Reynolds v. Sims of 1962 &1964 had the effect of ending the so called over-representation of rural areas in state legislatures, as well as the under-representation of suburbs. They did this by requiring state senates to be apportioned using a one man, one vote scheme. Warren declared "To the extent that a citizen's right to vote is debased, he is that much less a citizen…. The weight of a citizen's vote cannot be made to depend on where he lives. This is the clear and strong command of our Constitution's Equal Protection Clause." But of course there is no legitimate basis for this idea which is pure "Substantive Equal Protection". If any right is basic to our Constitution it is the guarantee of a Republican form of government including checks and balances. A senate based on equal representation for counties balanced the one man, one vote in the state house of representatives. My rural county doesn't have a single dual lane highway because we share a senator with a big city in the next county. That means our vote isn't even needed.

The Court prevented prosecutors from using evidence seized in illegal searches in Mapp v. Ohio in 1961. The Fourth Amendment certainly guarantees a right against unreasonable search and seizure. It does not provide a specific remedy for the violation of that right. There is nowhere to be found in the Constitution a requirement that an obviously guilty person must be set free when there is indisputable proof of guilt, especially in the case of a violent repeat offender. The Court, which does not have legislative authority, had written yet another unconstitutional volume of laws.

In Miranda v. Arizona in1966 Warren required police to issue a specific warning listing all of an accused individual's rights when making an arrest. The decision created a long list of specific rules for police questioning of suspects that reads more like a legislative statute than a judicial decision. And did we mention that the Court does not have the Constitutional power to write laws. Nor is it logical for anyone who has been read their rights a dozen times in the past to be set free if they were not read the thirteenth time. It is yet another case of a nice idea replacing Constitutional law.

Antitrust law was made into a joke as the Court ruled against almost every business defendant no matter what the precedent, economic reality, or the facts of the case.

Warren's Court also sought to redefine the First Amendment by outlawing mandatory school prayer in Engel v. Vitale in 1962. While many would agree with the policy it is certainly not required by the First Amendment as we shall see in the separate chapter on that Fraud.

One landmark case decided by the Court, Griswold v. Connecticut in 1965 discovered a constitutionally protected right of privacy, emanating from the "Due Process Clause" of the Fourteenth Amendment and "penumbras surrounding other Amendments, using (you'll never guess) our old friend/fraud "Substantive Due Process". This decision was fundamental, after Warren's retirement, to Roe v. Wade and discovery of the unconstitutional constitutional right of abortion.

From here on out we will bypass the historical timeline and address specific issues that came before the United States Supreme Court.

CHAPTER 13. - BROWN V. THE BOARD OF EDUCATION OR HOW TO CLAIM ORIGINAL UNDERSTANDING WOULD END DESEGREGATION

Brown v. Board of Education in 1954 was the landmark decision in Civil Rights law that ended segregation in the public schools. It was a correct decision but the opinion was a mess that implied the Justices were not at all sure it was legitimate.

In the 1896 case of Plessy v. Ferguson involving segregation on Railroad cars the Court had ruled that "Separate But Equal" met the requirements of the Equal Protection Clause of the Fourteenth Amendment.

The Warren Court overturned Plessy, but not on the basis of the Equal Protection Clause. They found that, "The history of the Fourteenth Amendment is inconclusive as to its intended effect on public education." It appears the Court accepted that Plessy made "Separate But Equal" settled law, so they had to make something up to get around it.

Therefore they went into the psychological effects on African-American children. "Does segregation of children in public schools solely on the basis of race, even though the physical facilities and other "tangible" factors may be equal, deprive the children of the minority group of equal educational opportunities? We believe that it does…. the policy of separating the races is usually interpreted as denoting the inferiority of the negro group. A sense of inferiority affects the motivation of a child to learn." Although the decision as written obviously could only apply to schools it was soon applied to other areas citing Brown even though it did not really apply.

It is this obvious misapplication of the law that has created problems for Originalists. Whenever the left wants to assault the legitimacy of Originalism they claim that its application would end desegregation, undermine the First Amendment, and Ban Abortions. While all of these claims are nonsense, we will discuss the other two in their own chapters.

The left claims that the original understanding of the Fourteenth Amendment, as explained in Plessy, supported "Separate But Equal". Therefore Originalists would have upheld segregation and would reinstate it if they controlled the Court. The charge is entirely consistent with the left's total inability to understand conservatism and their contention that all conservatives must be racist.

The truth is that Plessy determined that the original understanding of the "Equal Protection Clause" required racial equality. The fact that the Court thought "Separate But Equal" met the requirements of the "Equal Protection Clause" was an error based on the fact that the doctrine had hardly been tried or tested at the time of the decision.

By 1954 there had been literally hundreds of cases in lower courts that had proved beyond any shadow of a doubt that "Separate" was never "Equal".

Had Brown been decided on the basis of the actual Original Understanding it would have been a much better decision than the one based on the doublespeak the Court used as its excuse. It would seem that even when their decisions are actually constitutional the left has to find devious ways to justify them.

CHAPTER 14. - INCORPORATION OR OLD MCDONALD HAD A FRAUD

"The public welfare demands that constitutional cases must be decided according to the terms of the Constitution itself, and not according to judges' views of fairness, reasonableness, or justice." – Justice Hugo Black

In 1833 the Supreme Court had ruled that the Bill of Rights did not apply to the states. But in the 1920's the Court discovered that the "Substantive Due Process" fraud could be used to "Incorporate" the Bill of Rights onto the states.

It is only common sense to assume that if the Fourteenth Amendment applies the Bill of Rights onto the states then it would apply the entire Bill of Rights and apply it all in the same manner. Justice Hugo Black argued just that in the 1940's, but that would never be the consensus of the Court. They found it much easier to apply their politically correct views onto the states if they could pick and choose the parts of Bill of Rights that they liked and applied each in a different way that best supported their current political goal. It is yet another legal doctrine that doesn't pass the smell test.

This "Selective Incorporation" resorted to claiming that a state's action shocked the conscience of the Court or was inconsistent with the concept of "ordered liberty", or violated a "Fundamental Right" as opposed to the rights that they didn't favor. The Second Amendment was not considered "Fundamental" until 2011. Under this doctrine the Seventh Amendment right to a jury trial is still not considered "Fundamental."

Some of the most pernicious decisions of the court were derived from "Due Process" and "Selective Incorporation". In the next two chapters we will look at the damage done to just the First Amendment. Here, however, we are going to look at the Second Amendment case McDonald v. Chicago.

In this case the Court ruled that the Second Amendment applies to the States. The dissenters argued that "There has been, and is, no consensus that the right is, or was, "fundamental." And of course "Incorporation" only covers "Fundamental" rights. And only the elite left wing of the Court is supposed to know which rights are politically correct enough to be considered "Fundamental."

While the majority of five agreed that the Second Amendment applies to the states, Justice Thomas takes a different approach than the other Justices: "I agree with the Court that the Fourteenth Amendment makes the right to keep and bear arms set forth in the Second Amendment 'fully applicable to the States.' But I cannot agree that it is enforceable against the States through a clause that speaks only to 'process.' Instead, the right to keep and bear arms is a privilege of American citizenship that applies to the States through the Fourteenth Amendment's Privileges or Immunities Clause."

The other four so called "Conservative" Justices chose to base their "Incorporation" on the "Substantive Due Process" fraud. While I find some satisfaction in seeing their own fraud used against the liberal wing of the Court it is no less a fraud, and proves yet again that there is no right wing on this court.

The majority decision is in large part a history of the "Selective Incorporation" fraud used to explain how the Second Amendment is actually compatible with the fraudulent doctrine. The rest of this chapter is text from that decision. Much is deleted because it does not apply to the history of "Incorporation" or it is unnecessary material such as footnotes and references. It will give you a taste of judicial reasoning and doublespeak laced with enough bovine excrement to convince any reasonable person that the entire doctrine is nothing but made up garbage for reaching political goals. The entire text of the opinion can be easily found online.

SUPREME COURT OF THE UNITED STATES
No. 08–1521
OTIS MCDONALD, ET AL., PETITIONERS v. CITY OF CHICAGO, ILLINOIS, ET AL.
ON WRIT OF CERTIORARI TO THE UNITED STATES COURT OF APPEALS FOR THE SEVENTH CIRCUIT
[June 28, 2010]

JUSTICE ALITO announced the judgment of the Court and delivered the opinion of the Court with respect to Parts I, II–A, II–B, II–D, III–A, and III–B, in which THE CHIEF JUSTICE, JUSTICE SCALIA, JUSTICE KENNEDY, and JUSTICE THOMAS join, and an opinion with respect to Parts II–C, IV, and V, in which THE CHIEF JUSTICE, JUSTICE SCALIA, and JUSTICE KENNEDY join.

Two years ago, in District of Columbia v. Heller, 554 U. S. ___ (2008), we held that the Second Amendment protects the right to keep and bear arms for the purpose of self-defense, and we struck down a District of Columbia law that banned the possession of handguns in the home. The city of Chicago (City) and the village of Oak Park, a Chicago suburb, have laws that are similar to the District of Columbia's, but Chicago and Oak Park argue that their laws are constitutional because the Second Amendment has no application to the States. We have previously held that most of the provisions of the Bill of Rights apply with full force to both the Federal Government and the States. Applying the standard that is well established in our case law, we hold that the Second Amendment right is fully applicable to the States.

The Bill of Rights, including the Second Amendment, originally applied only to the Federal Government. In Barron ex rel. Tiernan v. Mayor of Baltimore, (1833), the Court, in an opinion by Chief Justice Marshall, explained that this question was "of great importance" but "not of much difficulty." In less than four pages, the Court firmly rejected the proposition that the first eight Amendments operate as limitations on the States, holding that they apply only to the Federal Government. ("[I]t is now settled that those amendments [in the Bill of Rights] do not extend to the states").

The constitutional Amendments adopted in the aftermath of the Civil War fundamentally altered our country's federal system. The provision at issue in this case, §1 of the Fourteenth Amendment, provides, among other things, that a State may not abridge "the privileges or immunities of citizens of the United States" or deprive "any person of life, liberty, or property, without due process of law."

Four years after the adoption of the Fourteenth Amendment, this Court was asked to interpret the Amendment's reference to "the privileges or immunities of citizens of the United States." The Slaughter-House Cases, supra, involved challenges to a Louisiana law permitting the creation of a state-sanctioned monopoly on the butchering of animals within the city of New Orleans. Justice Samuel Miller's opinion for the Court concluded that the Privileges or Immunities Clause protects only those rights "which owe their existence to the Federal government, its National character, its Constitution, or its laws." The Court held that other fundamental rights—rights that predated the creation of the Federal Government and that "the State governments were created to establish and secure"—were not protected by the Clause.

In drawing a sharp distinction between the rights of federal and state citizenship, the Court relied on two principal arguments. First, the Court emphasized that the Fourteenth Amendment's Privileges or Immunities Clause spoke of "the privileges or immunities of citizens of the United States," and the Court contrasted this phrasing with the wording in the first sentence of the Fourteenth Amendment and in the Privileges and Immunities Clause of Article IV, both of which refer to state citizenship. (Emphasis added.) Second, the Court stated that a contrary reading would "radically chang[e] the whole theory of the relations of the State and Federal governments to each other and of both these governments to the people," and the Court refused to conclude that such a change had been made "in the absence of language which expresses such a purpose too clearly to admit of doubt." Finding the phrase "privileges or immunities of citizens of the United States" lacking by this high standard, the Court reasoned that the phrase must mean something more limited.

Under the Court's narrow reading, the Privileges or Immunities Clause protects such things as the right

"to come to the seat of government to assert any claim [a citizen] may have upon that government, to transact any business he may have with it, to seek its protection, to share its offices, to engage in administering its functions . . . [and to] become a citizen of any State of the Union by a bonâ fide residence therein, with the same rights as other citizens of that State."

As previously noted, the Seventh Circuit concluded that Cruikshank, Presser, and Miller doomed petitioners' claims at the Court of Appeals level. Petitioners argue, however, that we should overrule those decisions and hold that the right to keep and bear arms is one of the "privileges or immunities of citizens of the United States." In petitioners' view, the Privileges or Immunities Clause protects all of the rights set out in the Bill of Rights, as well as some others, see Brief for Petitioners 10, 14, 15–21, but petitioners are unable to identify the Clause's full scope, Tr. of Oral Arg. 5–6, 8–11. Nor is there any consensus on that question among the scholars who agree that the Slaughter-House Cases' interpretation is flawed. (THOMAS, J., dissenting).We see no need to reconsider that interpretation here. For many decades, the question of the rights protected by the Fourteenth Amendment against state infringement has been analyzed under the Due Process Clause of that Amendment and not under the Privileges or Immunities Clause. We therefore decline to disturb the Slaughter-House holding. At the same time, however, this Court's decisions in Cruikshank, Presser, and Miller do not preclude us from considering whether the Due Process Clause of the Fourteenth Amendment makes the Second Amendment right binding on the States. None of those cases "engage[d] in the sort of Fourteenth Amendment inquiry required by our later cases." As explained more fully below, Cruikshank, Presser, and Miller all preceded the era in which the Court began the process of "selective incorporation" under the Due Process Clause, and we have never previously addressed the question whether the right to keep and bear arms applies to the States under that theory.

Indeed, Cruikshank has not prevented us from holding that other rights that were at issue in that case are binding on the States through the Due Process Clause. In Cruikshank, the Court held that the general "right of the people peaceably to assemble for lawful purposes," which is protected by the First Amendment, applied only against the Federal Government and not against the States. Nonetheless, over 60 years later the Court held that the right of peaceful assembly was a "fundamental righ[t] . . . safeguarded by the due process clause of the Fourteenth Amendment." De Jonge v. Oregon, (1937). We follow the same path here and thus consider whether the right to keep and bear arms applies to the States under the Due Process Clause.

In the late 19th century, the Court began to consider whether the Due Process Clause prohibits the States from infringing rights set out in the Bill of Rights. See Hurtado v. California, (1884) (due process does not require grand jury indictment); Chicago, B. & Q. R. Co. v. Chicago, (1897) (due process prohibits States from taking of private property for public use without just compensation). Five features of the approach taken during the ensuing era should be noted.

First, the Court viewed the due process question as entirely separate from the question whether a right was a privilege or immunity of national citizenship. See Twining v. New Jersey, (1908).

Second, the Court explained that the only rights protected against state infringement by the Due Process Clause were those rights "of such a nature that they are included in the conception of due process of law." While it was "possible that some of the personal rights safeguarded by the first eight Amendments against National action [might] also be safeguarded against state action," the Court stated, this was "not because those rights are enumerated in the first eight Amendments."

The Court used different formulations in describing the boundaries of due process. For example, in Twining, the Court referred to "immutable principles of justice which inhere in the very idea of free government which no member of the Union may disregard." In Snyder v. Massachusetts, (1934), the Court spoke of rights that are "so rooted in the traditions and conscience of our people as to be ranked as fundamental." And in Palko, the Court famously said that due process protects those rights that are "the very essence of a scheme of ordered liberty" and essential to "a fair and enlightened system of justice."

Third, in some cases decided during this era the Court" can be seen as having asked, when inquiring into whether some particular procedural safeguard was required of a State, if a civilized system could be imagined that would not accord the particular protection." Duncan v. Louisiana, (1968). Thus, in holding that due process prohibits a State from taking private property without just compensation, the Court described the right as "a principle of natural equity, recognized by all temperate and civilized governments, from a deep and universal sense of its justice." Chicago, B. & Q. R. Co. Similarly, the Court found that due process did not provide a right against compelled incrimination in part because this right "has no place in the jurisprudence of civilized and free countries outside the domain of the common law."

Fourth, the Court during this era was not hesitant to hold that a right set out in the Bill of Rights failed to meet the test for inclusion within the protection of the Due Process Clause. The Court found that some such rights qualified. See, e.g., Gitlow v. New York, (1925) (freedom of speech and press); Near v. Minnesota ex rel. Olson, (1931); Powell, supra (assistance of counsel in capital cases); De Jonge, supra (freedom of assembly); Cantwell v. Connecticut, (1940) (free exercise of religion). But others did not. See, e.g., Hurtado, (grand jury indictment requirement); Twining, (privilege against self-incrimination). Finally, even when a right set out in the Bill of Rights was held to fall within the conception of due process, the protection or remedies afforded against state infringement sometimes differed from the protection or remedies provided against abridgment by the Federal Government. To give one example, in Betts the Court held that, although the Sixth Amendment required the appointment of counsel in all federal criminal cases in which the defendant was unable to retain an attorney, the Due Process Clause required appointment of counsel in state criminal proceedings only where "want of counsel in [the] particular case. . . result[ed] in a conviction lacking in . . . fundamental fairness." Similarly, in Wolf v. Colorado, (1949), the Court held that the "core of the Fourth Amendment" was implicit in the concept of ordered liberty and thus "enforceable against the States through the Due Process Clause" but that the exclusionary rule, which applied in federal cases, did not apply to the States. An alternative theory regarding the relationship between the Bill of Rights and §1 of the Fourteenth Amendment was championed by Justice Black. This theory held that §1 of the Fourteenth Amendment totally incorporate all of the provisions of the Bill of Rights. Adamson (Black, J., dissenting); Duncan, (Black, J., concurring). As Justice Black noted, the chief congressional proponents of the Fourteenth Amendment espoused the view that the Amendment made the Bill of Rights applicable to the States and, in so doing, overruled this Court's decision in Barron.9 Adamson, (dissenting opinion).10 Nonetheless, the Court never has embraced Justice Black's "total incorporation" theory.

While Justice Black's theory was never adopted, the Court eventually moved in that direction by initiating what has been called a process of "selective incorporation," i.e., the Court began to hold that the Due Process Clause fully incorporates particular rights contained in the first eight Amendments.

Proponents of the view that §1 of the Fourteenth Amendment makes all of the provisions of the Bill of Rights applicable to the States respond that the terms privileges, immunities, and rights were used interchangeably at the time, and that the position taken by the leading congressional proponents of the Amendment was widely publicized and understood. Original Popular Understanding of the Fourteenth Amendment as Reflected in the Print Media of 1866–1868, 30 Whittier L. Rev. A number of scholars have found support for the total incorporation of the Bill of Rights.

The decisions during this time abandoned three of the previously noted characteristics of the earlier period.11 The Court made it clear that the governing standard is not whether any "civilized system [can] be imagined that would not accord the particular protection." Instead, the Court inquired whether a particular Bill of Rights guarantee is fundamental to our scheme of ordered liberty and system of justice. (referring to those "fundamental principles of liberty and justice which lie at the base of all our civil and political institutions).

The Court also shed any reluctance to hold that rights guaranteed by the Bill of Rights met the requirements for protection under the Due Process Clause. The Court eventually incorporated almost all of the provisions of the Bill of Rights.12 Only a handful of the Bill of Rights protections remain unincorporated.

Finally, the Court abandoned "the notion that the Fourteenth Amendment applies to the States only a watered down, subjective version of the individual guarantees of the Bill of Rights," stating that it would be "incongruous" to apply different standards "depending on whether the claim was asserted in a state or federal court." Instead, the Court decisively held that incorporated Bill of Rights protections "are all to be enforced against the States under the Fourteenth Amendment according to the same standards that protect those personal rights against federal encroachment."

Employing this approach, the Court overruled earlier decisions in which it had held that particular Bill of Rights guarantees or remedies did not apply to the States.

With this framework in mind, we now turn directly to the question whether the Second Amendment right to keep and bear arms is incorporated in the concept of due process. In answering that question, as just explained, we must decide whether the right to keep and bear arms is fundamental to our scheme of ordered liberty, or as we have said in a related context, whether this right is "deeply rooted in this Nation's history and tradition," Washington v. Glucksberg,

Our decision in Heller points unmistakably to the answer. Self-defense is a basic right, recognized by many legal systems from ancient times to the present day, and in Heller, we held that individual self-defense is "the central component" of the Second Amendment right.

Explaining that "the need for defense of self, family, and property is most acute" in the home, ibid., we found that this right applies to handguns because they are "the most preferred firearm in the nation to 'keep' and use for protection of one's home and family," "[T]he American people have considered the handgun to be the quintessential self-defense weapon"). Thus, we concluded, citizens must be permitted "to use [handguns] for the core lawful purpose of self-defense."

Heller makes it clear that this right is "deeply rooted in this Nation's history and tradition." Heller explored the right's origins, noting that the 1689 English Bill of Rights explicitly protected a right to keep arms for self defense, and that by 1765, Blackstone was able to assert that the right to keep and bear arms was "one of the fundamental rights of Englishmen," Blackstone's assessment was shared by the American colonists. As we noted in Heller, King George III's attempt to disarm the colonists in the 1760's and 1770's "provoked polemical reactions by Americans invoking their rights as Englishmen to keep arms."

The right to keep and bear arms was considered no less fundamental by those who drafted and ratified the Bill of Rights. "During the 1788 ratification debates, the fear that the federal government would disarm the people in order to impose rule through a standing army or select militia was pervasive in Antifederalist rhetoric."

From this point in their opinion the Court continued to explain why the

Second Amendment was a "Fundamental Right" that qualified for incorporation under the fraudulent doctrine of "Substantive Due Process." The entire text of the opinion and dissents are easily found online.

Only the "extreme right wing" Justice Thomas proposed a legitimate common sense Constitutional solution for applying the Second Amendment and the entire Bill of Rights to the States.

"We should not forget that the spark which ignited the American Revolution was caused by the British attempt to confiscate the firearms of the colonists." - Patrick Henry

CHAPTER 15. - WILL THE REAL FIRST AMENDMENT PLEASE STAND UP

"I have no fear of constitutional amendments properly adopted, but I do fear the rewriting of the Constitution by judges under the guise of interpretation." - Justice Hugo Black

The First Amendment is an elegant, concise, and masterfully written statement which Reads, "Congress shall make no law respecting an establishment of religion, or prohibiting the free exercise thereof; or abridging the freedom of speech, or of the press; or the right of the people peaceably to assemble, and to petition the Government for a redress of grievances." It was written by legal scholars and men schooled in the proper use of English grammar which has been long forgotten by most people today. It was written by men who actually intended their words to mean exactly what they said.

Perhaps one of the reasons that the Constitution is rarely taught or understood is that, thanks to the Courts, it no longer means anything even vaguely resembling what it actually says. There have been numerous attempts to rewrite the First Amendment to actually say what it currently means. What better way to prove the low level of integrity and lack of respect that our Court's deserve. I will therefore add my feeble attempt to that of others before me.

Neither Congress, nor state legislatures, nor local governments, nor school boards shall make any laws, rules, or recommendations supporting and/or permitting establishments of religion, or allowing prayer in schools, or the bowing of heads that might be thought to be prayer in schools, nor are any religious artifacts, ideas, or symbols to be displayed on public property unless they are proved to have a secular reason, nor shall the word Jesus be used in prayers by state legislatures, nor shall the large body of laws written on this subject by the Courts, who have no authority to write laws, be considered to be in violation of any of these restrictions; Neither Congress nor state legislatures shall make any laws prohibiting the free exercise of religion except on public property; Neither Congress nor state legislatures may make any laws abridging the freedom of speech unless it is political speech within 60 days of an election (This section voided by the Court in 2011) or be political or other speech that a majority of the Court doesn't like with the definition of speech to include public nudity and pornography (subject to numerous limitations and exclusion known only to the court, but not to include virtual child pornography or flag burning which is actually speech); Neither Congress nor state legislatures shall make any laws abridging freedom of the press, or the internet, or TV except that it is ok to require equal time be given to both sides of an issue and the FCC can ban nudity and bad words sort of maybe, and reporters can be jailed for keeping sources confidential; Neither Congress nor state legislatures shall abridge the right of the people peaceably to assemble except that you can be jailed if you get too close to a public official under secret service protection (The last provision not yet approved by the court) and, absent a compelling governmental interest, political parties shall have absolute freedom from interference in their internal affairs except that the government can dictate how their candidates are selected; Neither Congress nor state legislatures shall abridge the right of the people to petition the Government for a redress of grievances unless you try to reach a member of Congress who is not in your district by e-mail; All of the above subject to whatever whims, modifications, improvements, restrictions, or revisions the United States Supreme Court may decide to invent.

In an Article in the University of Chicago Law Review entitled " Private Speech, Public Purpose: The Role of Governmental Motive in First Amendment Doctrine." Justice Kagan argued that the government has the right, even considering the First Amendment, to restrict free speech, when it believes the speech is "harmful", as long as the restriction is done with good intentions.

Justice Kagan's name was also on a brief, United States V. Stevens, found by the Washington Examiner, stating: "Whether a given category of speech enjoys First Amendment protection depends upon a categorical balancing of the value of the speech against its societal costs."

Justice Hugo Black tells us that "The Framers [of the Constitution] knew that free speech is the friend of change and revolution. But they also knew that it is always the deadliest enemy of tyranny."

CHAPTER 16. – THE ESTABLISHMENT CLAUSE OR WHAT PART OF "CONGRESS SHALL MAKE NO LAW" DON'T THEY UNDERSTAND

"... any broad unlimited power to hold laws unconstitutional because they offend what this Court conceives to be the 'conscience of our people' ... was not given by the Framers, but rather has been bestowed on the Court by the Court." – Justice Hugo Black

On February 18, 2004 I had the following article published on several web sites including Renew America (www.RenewAmerica.com). It reveals a side of the establishment clause that most people have never heard of before, and proves that the clause was actually supposed to mean exactly what it says.

The real First Amendment

With the Supreme Court considering the Ninth Circuit Court ban on "under God" in the Pledge of Allegiance and refusing to hear the case about Judge Roy Moore and his Ten Commandments Monument, perhaps it is time to take a fresh look at the First Amendment.

If the First Amendment read "Congress shall make no law respecting (regarding) jelly beans" there would be no question of the meaning.

It would be obvious that a law creating a federal jelly bean monopoly would be a violation of the law. Everyone would understand that Congress could not tax jelly beans, regulate jelly beans, ban jelly beans, or even write a law defining jelly beans. The Constitution would clearly ban any Federal interference with state jelly bean laws. It would also ban Federal interference with any personal use of jelly beans on public property.

If the Supreme Court tried to write laws regulating the use of jelly beans at the state or personal level it would be an obvious violation of the ban on Federal interference with state jelly bean laws. Someone might even remember that the Supreme Court has no Constitutional authority to write laws in the first place.

So why, when we substitute the words "establishment of religion" for jelly beans, do we suddenly lose the ability to see the obvious? Perhaps it is because we can't imagine a time when there would have been state establishments for the First Amendment to protect.

James Madison introduced the first draft, which read "nor shall any national religion be established." The meaning was clear and obvious. In conference committee the politicians in Congress changed the text to read, "Congress shall make no law respecting (pertaining to) an establishment of religion." What if they actually meant exactly what they said?

At the time the Bill of Rights was written and ratified, four or more of the eleven states had established religions depending on the definition used. Others had close relationships between church and state. Many of the Congressmen who wrote the Bill of Rights represented states that had tax supported religions and, like all politicians, wanted to protect the interests of their states. It would have been impossible to pass the First Amendment by a two-thirds vote without the support of some of these politicians. If you had lived in one of these states and read the words "Congress shall make no law" you would undoubtedly have concluded that Congress was banned from making any laws which would in any way affect your state establishment. If you were a congressman from one of these states it would be obvious that you intended those words to protect your state establishment from any federal interference. Even the Congressmen favoring the total separation of church and state would probably have had no objection to this more restrictive language since they wanted the federal government completely out of the religion business and the amendment only applied to the federal government.

Most people don't realize that Madison actually wrote two First Amendments, one for the federal government and one for the states, which was not passed by Congress. His version for the states did not include an establishment clause.

It appears that the final language of the establishment clause was written at least in part to protect state establishments from any federal interference. Therefore, the entire body of law written by the federal courts "respecting an establishment of religion" is in direct violation of the First Amendment, which clearly bans the federal government from interfering with state establishments of religion.

It could be argued that this no longer applies because there are no more state establishments of religion. But then, of course, we all know that is false. We have over fifty years of case law telling us that establishments are lurking everywhere. They are hiding under school desks, behind nativity scenes on public property, on school vouchers, in the Pledge of Allegiance, and, according to the ACLU, even on school calendars listing a terrible establishment called Christmas vacation. And the First Amendment declares every one of these establishments off limits to the federal government. It is the letter of the law, the original understanding of the law, and obviously the original intent of the law.

This produces a real Constitutional paradox. How can you "Incorporate" a clause onto the states banning state establishments when the "Original Intent" of the clause was to protect state establishments and guarantee state legislatures the sole right to regulate establishments? The rest of the First Amendment can be easily incorporated as "The State Legislatures Shall Make No Law", but that won't work with the Establishment Clause. If applied to the states the word "respecting" (pertaining to) creates two conflicting requirements that cancel each other out and leave the Courts with no authority over religion at the state level whatsoever.

It was Judge Black in Everson v. Board of Education who first ruled "the clause against establishment of religion by law was intended to erect 'a wall of separation between Church and State.'"

CHAPTER 17. – PENUMBRAS OR WHY NO OTHER DRUG BUT CONTRACEPTIVES NEED APPLY FOR PRIVACY PROTECTION

"[The Fourth Amendment's framers] had a specific principle of privacy at work in the Fourth Amendment. It was privacy in your home and in your office from search by the government. That is not just a broad ranging right of privacy you can apply anywhere. Now, [Justice William] Douglas made up a right of privacy that's attached to nothing." - Judge Robert Bork

Even though "Substantive Due Process" gives the Court a license to invent rights and legislate from the bench, they are still faced with one major problem to solve; they still need to make their decision sound legitimate with excuses that appear both plausible and legal. They found one such excuse in 1965.

The state of Connecticut had an ancient law banning contraceptives and another punishing people who help others break the law. No one had ever been charged with this crime, but the left wanted to make it an issue. In order to even get it in court they had to talk a prosecutor into charging two doctors with the crime and impose a $100 fine.

When the case reached the Supreme Court Justice Douglas took the opportunity to invent an entirely new "Right of Privacy" completely out of thin air.

Regarding a law that had never been enforced and probably never would be he said, "Would we allow the police to search the sacred precincts of marital bedrooms for telltale signs of the use of contraceptives? The very idea is repulsive to the notions of privacy surrounding the marriage relationship." This statement is totally irrelevant to the issue and is, in any case, forbidden by the Fourth Amendment prohibition "against unreasonable searches and seizures."

Douglas pointed out that "specific guarantees in the Bill of Rights have penumbras, formed by emanations from those guarantees that give them life and substance." Judge Bork tells us that this is not an unusual concept except for the terminology. That in fact the Court sometimes creates a buffer zone around a specific right if it believes that an action is likely to create a violation of the right. However, these buffer zones are tightly tailored to protect specific rights that are actually in the Constitution.

But Douglas doesn't stop there. He found "zones of privacy" in the First Amendment, the Third Amendment which forbids the quartering of soldiers in private homes, the Fourth Amendment ban on unreasonable searches, and the Fifth Amendment ban on self-incrimination.

No logical buffer zones around the named rights, no matter how far you extend them, are relevant to the sale of contraceptive drugs. Douglas gets around this by declaring that the "zones of privacy" of the separate amendments somehow combine to create a totally undefined "right of privacy" that is independent of and lies outside any right or "zone of privacy" in the Constitution, and guarantees anything a majority of the Justices declare as politically correct.

As proof that this doctrine is bogus we only need to ask ourselves what other classes of drugs are protected by the privacy right. Terminal cancer patients have no constitutional right to medical marijuana or enough morphine to adequately control their pain. Viagra is not a constitutional right. And why not have a right to use heroin or cocaine in the privacy of your own bedroom? The truth is that no other class of drugs need apply because this is not a real right. It is nothing more than another judicial excuse to invent a politically correct law.

Judge Bork tells us "It is important to understand Justice Douglas's argument both because the method, though without merit, continually recurs in constitutional adjudication and because the "right of privacy" has become a loose cannon in the law"

Justice Black's dissent gets it one hundred percent correct; "I like my privacy as well as the next one, but I am nevertheless compelled to admit that the government has the right to invade it unless prohibited by a specific constitutional provision."

CHAPTER 18. – THE ABORTION BAN DIVIDES THE COUNTRY AS NEVER SINCE THE CIVIL WAR

George Will calls it "the "living"—actually, disappearing – Constitution."

"I've noticed that everybody that is for abortion has already been born."
- Ronald Reagan, quoted in New York Times, 22 September 1980

We often hear complaints about how divided our country is. While blame is often placed on liberal or conservative extremists, Congress, the President, or any of a dozen other groups, I believe a large part of the problem started with the polarization caused by the Supreme Court creating settled law on issues that should have been left to the legislatures to settle with debate, education, and compromise. This effect is even worse when a majority of people on both sides of the issue know that the Court's decision has no legitimate basis in law or the Constitution.

Abortion is just such an issue. Since the Court declared a right to abortion in 1973 both sides of the issue have been at war. With "settled law" there can be no more compromise on the issue, which was actually starting to occur at the time. The result is that both sides lose.

Pro-abortion advocates, (pro-choice is the right to choose between Colt, Ruger, or Smith and Wesson) get to live in fear of allowing honest judges on the Court because they would return the issue to the states where it constitutionally belongs. Their unconstitutional demand on the Court forces them to advocate for dishonest judges which undermines the integrity of the entire judicial system. They also lose all of the advances that their cause might have won through forty years of legitimate compromise.

Anti-abortion advocates are denied their constitutional right to petition for legislation that they support and that might have stopped the murder of millions of innocent babies. They also lose all of the advances that their cause might have won through forty years of legitimate compromise.

The issue has driven a giant wedge between the people on both sides of the debate, created a political class dependent on fighting for "Reproductive Rights," and has led to an ever increasing politicization of the Courts as we shall see in the next chapter. Short of slavery there has never been a more divisive issue in the United States.

Another result has been the creation of a Court that has lost the respect of everyone who takes the time to understand what they have actually done and those who don't but still know in their hearts that something about the Court's decisions smells of putrefaction. One wonders how these Justices and judges can subvert the law, ignore their oath, and still retain even a shred of self-respect or integrity.

Griswold v. Connecticut, (1965) created the "right of privacy" used to legalize abortion in Roe v. Wade, (1973).

In 1969 Norma McCorvey, under the alias Jane Roe, filed suit in a U.S. District Court in Texas asking to be allowed to have an abortion. She won in the District Court and the case eventually reached the Supreme Court where the Court extended the "Right of Privacy" to cover abortion. Strange that a surgical procedure performed in a hospital is considered private, but even stranger is the fact that no other surgical procedure is covered or considered a constitutional right, but that is how it works when a "right" is based solely on the judge's personal version of political correctness.

In order to justify the decision Justice Blackmum wrote a 51 page opinion that lacks any legitimate legal argument. He starts with an explanation of the statute involved and a lengthy history of abortion and abortion laws from the Persians and the Greeks till today, not one word of which is relevant to constitutional law.

Blackmum finally gets down to business saying "The Constitution does not explicitly mention any right of privacy." Then he follows with the excuses "the Court has recognized that a right of personal privacy, or a guarantee of certain areas or zones of privacy, does exist under the Constitution." And adds "These decisions make it clear that only personal rights that can be deemed "fundamental" or implicit in the concept of ordered liberty, are included in the guarantee of the right of privacy." And now we have added "fundamental rights" to the litany of Court doublespeak.

The decision was then settled with a statement which does not even address a specific place in the Constitution where the right to an abortion is to be found; "This right of privacy, whether it be founded in the Fourteenth Amendment's concept of personal liberty and restrictions upon state action, as we feel it is, or, as the District Court determined, in the Ninth Amendment's reservation of rights to the people, is broad enough to encompass a woman's decision whether or not to terminate her pregnancy."

The Court then wrote the legislation which spelled out the rules for the regulation of abortion. That the power of the Court to write legislation is nowhere to be found in the Constitution was no deterrent to Blackmum.

Justice White's dissent says it all: "I find nothing in the language or history of the Constitution to support the Courts judgment. The Court simply fashions and announces a new constitutional right for pregnant mothers and, with scarcely any reason or authority for its action, invests that right with sufficient substance to override most existing state abortion statutes.... As an exercise of raw judicial power, the Court perhaps has the authority to do what it does today; but in my view is an improvident and extravagant exercise of the power of judicial review that the Constitution extends to this Court."

Norma McCorvey became a member of the pro-life movement in 1995 and she now supports making abortion illegal.

Judge Bork notes that each year there are massive marches by pro-abortionists and anti-abortionists. "There the demonstrators march past the house of congress with hardly a glance and go straight to the Supreme Court building to make their moral sentiments known where they perceive those sentiments to be relevant.... So far as they are concerned, however, the primary political branch of government, to which they must address their petitions, is the Supreme Court. There is something very disturbing about those marches, for, if the marchers correctly perceive reality, and I think it undeniable that they do, a major heresy has entered into the American constitutional system.... **it is the introduction of the denial that judges are bound by law.**"

CHAPTER 19. - LAWRENCE V TEXAS IS THE RATIONAL EXTENSION OF THE PRIVACY RIGHT

In the 1986 case Bowers v. Hardwick, the Supreme Court upheld a challenged Georgia sodomy statute because it could not find a constitutional protection of sexual privacy. However, in the 2003 case Lawrence v. Texas they struck down a Texas state law that prohibited intimate sexual contact between members of the same sex. The Court declared that the "Texas statute furthers no legitimate state interest which can justify its intrusion into the personal and private life of the individual." The Court held that intimate consensual sexual conduct was part of the liberty protected by "Substantive Due Process" under the Fourteenth Amendment. Justice Kennedy cited the "Right of Privacy" from Griswold as the starting point in their decision. And he wrote, "The petitioners [Lawrence and Garner] are entitled to respect for their private lives. The State cannot demean their existence or control their destiny by making their private sexual conduct a crime."

Justice O'Connor, who wrote a concurring opinion, and framed it as an issue of "Rational Basis" review.

Generally when the Court decides that an unconstitutional law is constitutional (as in Affirmative Action) it applies what it calls "Strict Scrutiny". It is the strongest standard of judicial review that courts use to weigh the government's interest against a constitutional right or principle.

To pass "strict scrutiny" and sound like a good excuse to unconstitutionally override the Constitution, the law must satisfy three tests.

• It must be justified by a compelling governmental interest.
• The law must be narrowly tailored to achieve that goal or interest.
• And the law must be the least restrictive means for achieving that interest.

I have read the entire Constitution and can find no place in the document that allows ignoring the Constitution for a "Compelling Governmental Interest."

"Rational Basis" is the lowest level of scrutiny that a court applies when engaging in judicial review and does not usually apply in situations where a specific protected classification or a fundamental right is involved. It says that Congress is required to have a rational basis for legislation that, without it, might violate a right of a person under the Constitution's Fourteenth Amendment "Equal Protection Clause." Congress is not necessarily required to have a good reason as long as the legislative reasoning is not too arbitrary.

A court applying "Rational Basis" review will virtually always uphold a challenged law unless every proffered justification for it is grossly illogical. In this case a law based on morality is considered to be grossly illogical. This is a position that is totally offensive to anyone with religious values and it ignores the simple fact that virtually every decision made by a legislature is based at some level on the moral values of the representatives.

In his dissent Justice Scalia referenced the majority's lack of respect for "Stare Decisis" by overturning Bowers, noting that the same logic they used to overturn Bowers could be used to overturn Roe v. Wade. He also indicated that if the court was not prepared to approve laws based on moral choices as it had done in Bowers, then state laws against things like bigamy, same-sex marriage, prostitution, adultery, obscenity, and bestiality could also be overturned.

Several quotes from his dissent read: "Today's opinion is the product of a Court, which is the product of a law-profession culture, that has largely signed on to the so-called homosexual agenda. ...the Court has taken sides in the culture war, departing from its role of assuring, as neutral observer, that the democratic rules of engagement are observed.... So imbued is the Court with the law profession's anti-anti-homosexual culture, that it is seemingly unaware that the attitudes of that culture are not obviously 'mainstream.'"

Justice Thomas, as usual, was blunter in his dissent. He wrote that the law struck down was "uncommonly silly", but he voted to uphold it because he could find "no general right of privacy" in the Constitution. He added that if he was a member of the Texas legislature he would vote to repeal the law.

"The Constitution does not prohibit legislatures from enacting stupid laws." - Thurgood Marshall

So now the Court not only has another illegitimate excuse for overturning a law, it has yet another political constituency for dishonest judges.

CHAPTER 20. - THE "BORKING" OF THE SUPREME COURT

"Roe, as the greatest example and symbol of the judicial usurpation of the democratic prerogatives in this century, should be overturned." – Judge Bork

When Justice Powell retired, President Reagan announced the nomination of Judge Robert Bork to the Supreme Court: "Judge Bork is recognized as a premier constitutional authority. His outstanding intellect and unrivaled scholarly credentials are reflected in his thoughtful examination of the broad, fundamental legal issues of our times. When confirmed by the Senate as an appellate judge in 1982, the American bar association gave him its highest rating: exceptionally well qualified. …He'll bring credit to the Court and his colleague, as well as to his country and the Constitution"

Following Bork's nomination to the Court Sen. Ted Kennedy trashed the judge with his famous "Robert Bork's America" speech: "Robert Bork's America is a land in which women would be forced into back-alley abortions, blacks would sit at segregated lunch counters, rogue police could break down citizens' doors in midnight raids, schoolchildren could not be taught about evolution, writers and artists could be censored at the whim of the Government, and the doors of the Federal courts would be shut on the fingers of millions of citizens for whom the judiciary is—and is often the only—protector of the individual rights that are the heart of our democracy … No justice would be better than this injustice."

Bork responded that, "There was not a line in that speech that was accurate." However, with the help of the American Civil Liberties Union, a liberal press, feminist groups, and TV adds by Gregory Peck it worked.

Senator Grassley commented "Make no mistake about it, the critics of this; (sic) nominee know the law they prefer is judge-made, and therefore susceptible to change by other judges. Their loud protests underscore that the law they prefer is not found in the Constitution or the statutes."

Based primarily on his stand that there is no "right of privacy" in the

Constitution, an opinion that threatened the "right of abortion" found in Roe, all of the advocates for dishonest judges came out in force and killed Bork's nomination to the Court.

In March 2002, the Oxford English Dictionary added an entry for the verb Bork as U.S. political slang, with this definition: "To defame or vilify (a person) systematically, esp. in the mass media, usually with the aim of preventing his or her appointment to public office; to obstruct or thwart (a person) in this way."

One of the best known uses of the verb to bork occurred in July 1991 at a conference of the National Organization for Women when feminist Florynce Kennedy addressed the conference on the importance of defeating the nomination of Clarence Thomas to the U.S. Supreme Court. She said, "We're going to bork him. We're going to kill him politically ... This little creep, where did he come from?" Thomas, the only real moderate Justice on the Court, was later confirmed after another of the most divisive confirmation hearings in Supreme Court history.

When Ruth Bader Ginsberg was nominated to the Court, Indiana Senator Richard Lugar and then Senator Biden convinced the Judiciary committee that they should not ask any questions regarding how the candidate would vote on an issue. Lugar later stated that this self-imposed senatorial ignorance of the judge's position on the issues would somehow lead to Justices being more impartial and honest on the bench. They then convinced the Republicans in the Senate to overwhelmingly vote to confirm the most extreme left wing Justice on the Court on the totally unfounded idea that the advocates for judicial dishonesty would reciprocate and vote for honest judges when they were nominated.

Lugar's prescription for senatorial ignorance continues to this day. Presidents try to nominate judges who share their own political persuasion but don't have enough of an official, provable position on abortion, and nominees refuse to answer any direct questions on the issue. This allows Senators to claim ignorance when they vote on confirmation which was, of course, the real reason for Lugar's "ignorance doctrine." The TEA Parties in Indiana orchestrated the six term Senator's 2012 primary loss in part because of his votes to confirm dishonest, left wing, extremist nominees Ruth Bader Ginsberg, Sonia Sodomayor, and Elena Kagan to the Court.

"The tactics and techniques of national political campaigns have been unleashed on the process of confirming judges. That is not simply disturbing. It is dangerous." – Judge Robert Bork

But it is the natural progression of things when the Court makes decisions that are understood by the general public to be blatantly political rather than legal.

CHAPTER 21. – "WINE"ING ABOUT AN OBVIOUS FRAUD

"Why don't they pass a constitutional amendment prohibiting anybody from learning anything? If it works as well as prohibition did, in five years Americans would be the smartest race of people on Earth." - Will Rogers

On May 16, 2005 the Supreme Court issued its 5-4 opinion in Granholm v. Heald and consolidated cases. It ruled that Michigan's and New York's regulatory schemes that permit in state wineries to directly ship alcohol to consumers, but restrict the ability of out-of-state wineries to do so, violates the commerce clause.

This little known, obscure case is of interest to us because it illustrates the complete disingenuousness of the Court in an extremely easy to understand manner.

Section 2 of the 21st Amendment which repeals prohibition reads as follows: "The transportation or importation into any State, Territory, or possession of the United States for delivery or use therein of intoxicating liquors, in violation of the laws thereof, is hereby prohibited." Simply put it prohibits importation of alcoholic beverages into a state in violation of that state's laws.

The Supreme Court stated that "both States discriminate against interstate commerce in violation of the Commerce Clause, Art. I, §8, cl. 3, and that the discrimination is neither authorized nor permitted by the Twenty-first Amendment. Accordingly, we affirm the judgment of the Court of Appeals for the Sixth Circuit, which invalidated the Michigan laws; and we reverse the judgment of the Court of Appeals for the Second Circuit, which upheld the New York laws." It added that "The differential treatment between in state and out of state wineries constitutes explicit discrimination against interstate commerce." And it concluded that "Without demonstrating the need for discrimination, New York and

Michigan have enacted regulations that disadvantage out-of-state wine producers. Under our Commerce Clause jurisprudence, these regulations cannot stand."

In short they have ruled that the interstate commerce clause trumps the 21st Amendment. I have to ask "What part of "Amendment" don't they understand. An amendment is defined as "The process of formally altering or adding to a document or record." This ruling would be like saying that women can't vote because the original Constitution trumps the 19th Amendment.

Justice Stevens' dissent stated "The New York and Michigan laws challenged in these cases would be patently invalid under well settled dormant Commerce Clause principles if they regulated sales of an ordinary article of commerce rather than wine. But ever since the adoption of the Eighteenth Amendment and the Twenty-first Amendment, our Constitution has placed commerce in alcoholic beverages in a special category."

In his separate dissent Justice Thomas argued "In sum, the Webb-Kenyon Act authorizes the discriminatory state laws before the Court today." And he said that even if the Webb-Kenyon Act did not exist, a proper reading of the 21st Amendment shows that it was meant to permit states to enact these sorts of restrictions.

It is such a simple concept that it took 73 pages for the Justices to explain why an Amendment can be overturned by something in the body of the original Constitution. Online shopping received a substantial boost with this ruling, but the integrity of the Court took another hit.

"The public welfare demands that constitutional cases must be decided according to the terms of the Constitution itself, and not according to judges' views of fairness, reasonableness, or justice." – Justice Hugo Black

CHAPTER 22. – AFFIRMATIVE ACTION IS UNCONSTITUTIONAL – SORT OF MAYBE

"I have no fear of constitutional amendments properly adopted, but I do fear the rewriting of the Constitution by judges under the guise of interpretation." – Justice Hugo Black

In 1964 President Johnson, who had blocked Republican civil rights legislation as Democratic Senate Majority Leader, signed the Civil Rights Act of 1964. While it was debated in Congress its sponsors swore that it would never be used to promote reverse discrimination. The Supreme Court soon made a lie out of that promise.

Title VII of the Civil Rights Act of 1964 states "It shall be unlawful employment practice for an employer to fail or refuse to hire or to discharge any individual, or otherwise discriminate against any individual with respect to his compensation, terms, conditions, or privileges of employment, because of such individual's race, color, religion, sex, or national origin." One would hardly think that those words could be used to require discrimination based on race. That is unless one understands that many Supreme Court Justices are dishonest purveyors of political correctness.

In 1973 Griggs v. Duke Power Co. black employees challenged the requirement of a high school diploma for certain jobs. The Court ruled that, even though no discrimination was intended, because more whites were promoted it was a violation of the statute. Companies now adopted quotas in self-defense.

In 1979 United Steelworkers of America v. Weber, Brian Weber was passed over in favor of several black workers with less seniority because of a quota system. The court held that since the purpose of the act was to break down barriers to black employment Congress couldn't have meant to prevent preferential treatment for blacks. Of course the first statement does not lead logically to the second. This legal theory is called "Purposive Interpretation" or as Scalia calls it "purposivism."

Critics of purposivism argue it fails to recognize the separation of powers between the legislature and the judiciary. Regardless of the overall purpose behind legislation, it was the legislature that determined, by what they wrote, exactly how they wanted that purpose to be executed. Since "Purposive Interpretation" goes beyond the words within the statute, considerable power is bestowed upon the judges to write new laws that they think the legislature might have preferred instead of what they actually enacted into law. And the power of the courts to write legislation is nowhere to be found in the Constitution.

In Johnson v. Transportation Agency, Santa Clara County, despite no evidence of any discrimination, Diane Joyce was promoted over Johnson, who scored higher in the job interview, strictly because she was a woman. The Court ruled that such a plan was consistent with the Act.

It was now legal to discriminate against someone who had not discriminated in order to help someone who was not a victim of discrimination. The transformation of the law was complete despite both the letter of the law and the promises of its supporters in Congress.

Those who advocated a color blind society in the 60's now call advocates of a color blind society bigots.

In July 2003 the US Supreme Court in Grutter v. Bollinger ruled that reverse discrimination was OK at the University of Michigan as long as there were no specific quotas. The Fourteenth Amendment reads in part "nor deny to any person within its jurisdiction the equal protection of the laws." Justice O'Conner apparently never read that part of the Amendment.

Justice O'Connor wrote, "It follows from that principle that 'government may treat people differently because of their race only for the most compelling reasons'... This means that such classifications are constitutional only if they are narrowly tailored to further compelling governmental interests."

She also stated that "race-conscious admissions policies must be limited in time.... The Court takes the Law School at its word that it would like nothing better than to find a race-neutral admissions formula and will terminate its use of racial preferences as soon as practicable. The Court expects that 25 years from now, the use of racial preferences will no longer be necessary to further the interest approved today."

The majority of the US Supreme Court has not only stated that it is OK for the government and the Court to ignore the Civil Rights Act and the Fourteenth Amendment if they have a good reason, but that they can do it for another twenty five years. If the Court can ignore the Constitution whenever it wants and for as long as it wants, then what rights does the

Constitution actually guarantee?

And the Court has now found yet another major political constituency for dishonest judges.

"Equal treatment and equality before the law—these are the foundations on which a just and free society is built. But there are some today who, in the name of equality, would have us practice discrimination. They have turned our civil rights laws on their head, claiming they mean exactly the opposite of what they say." - President Ronald Reagan

CHAPTER 23. - KELO V. CITY OF NEW LONDON OR HOW TO TAKE FROM THE POOR AND GIVE TO THE RICH

"Something has gone seriously awry with this Court's interpretation of the Constitution. Though citizens are safe from the government in their homes, the homes themselves are not." – Justice Thomas

The Fifth Amendment reads: "No person shall be held to answer for a capital, or otherwise infamous crime, unless on a presentment or indictment of a Grand Jury, except in cases arising in the land or naval forces, or in the Militia, when in actual service in time of War or public danger; nor shall any person be subject for the same offense to be twice put in jeopardy of life or limb; nor shall be compelled in any criminal case to be a witness against himself, nor be deprived of life, liberty, or property, without due process of law; nor shall private property be taken for public use, without just compensation."

Kelo v. City of New London, (2005) was a case in which the city of New London used eminent domain to transfer land from one private owner to another private owner to further economic development. In a 5–4 decision, the Court held that the general benefits a community enjoyed from economic growth qualified private redevelopment plans as a permissible "public use" under the Takings Clause of the Fifth Amendment. By the time the case was decided the developer was unable to obtain financing and the now empty lot became a temporary dump.

Kelo's attorneys argued that economic development did not qualify as a "public use" under the Fifth Amendment. They said that it was not constitutional for the government to take private property from a private owner and give it to another private owner, if the government was simply doing so because it would put the property to a use that would generate higher tax revenue.

The state court held that if an economic project will create new jobs, increase tax and other city revenues, and revitalize a depressed urban area (even if that area is not blighted), then the project serves a "public purpose", which qualifies as a "public use".

In 2005 the Supreme Court's left wing, in a 5–4 decision, ruled in favor of the City of New London upholding the idea that "public purpose" is the same as "public use." This was not the first time "public use" had been interpreted by the Supreme Court as "public purpose". The Fifth Amendment was interpreted the same way in other earlier eminent domain cases. However, in those earlier cases, the court justified the use of eminent domain on the basis of elimination of social problems such as barriers to efficient use of agricultural and mineral-bearing land or the elimination of slums. None of these factors were present in Kelo. It was a case in which the city merely wanted to increase its tax revenue.

Justice O'Connor in her dissent argued that the decision eliminates "any distinction between private and public use of property — and thereby effectively delete[s] the words 'for public use' from the Takings Clause of the Fifth Amendment." Justice Thomas commenting on the same change in definition stated "This deferential shift in phraseology enables the Court to hold, against all common sense, that a costly urban-renewal project whose stated purpose is a vague promise of new jobs and increased tax revenue, but which is also suspiciously agreeable to the Pfizer Corporation, is for a 'public use.'"

Justice Thomas added "Allowing the government to take property solely for public purposes is bad enough, but extending the concept of public purpose to encompass any economically beneficial goal guarantees that these losses will fall disproportionately on poor communities. Those communities are not only systematically less likely to put their lands to the highest and best social use, but are also the least politically powerful."

"The true foundation of republican government is the equal right of every citizen in his person and property and in their management." – Thomas Jefferson

Economists almost universally agree that the biggest difference between successful economies and third world countries is strong private property rights. Unless people are secure in their rights regarding property ownership there is little incentive to invest in or start businesses.

There was considerable public outrage at this perversion of the Fifth Amendment which would be to benefit large corporations at the expense of individual homeowners and local communities. So much so that many states took steps to protect their citizens from this outrageous decision that unilaterally rewrote the word "use" to actually mean "purpose." Obviously the majority had not considered any of the basic principles of "Textualism".

Prior to Kelo only seven states specifically prohibited the use of eminent domain for economic development except to eliminate blight. As of 2012, 44 states had enacted legislation in response to the Kelo decision. Of those states, 22 enacted laws that significantly restricted takings allowed by Kelo, while the rest passed laws that placed at least some limits on the power of cities to take property for economic development.

"No other rights are safe where property is not safe." - Daniel Webster

CHAPTER 24. - BUSH V. GORE OR LIBERAL JUSTICES GORED ON "SUBSTANTIVE EQUAL PROTECTION"

"Well, I guess the one that created the most waves of disagreement was Bush v. Gore," says Scalia, referring to the Supreme Court decision on the 2000 presidential election. "That comes up all the time, and my usual response is 'get over it.'"

The 2000 Presidential Election in Florida was a major disaster that made us the laughing stock of the entire world, almost created a Constitutional crisis, still has many questioning the legitimacy of Bush's presidency, and has others claiming that the election was decided by a Republican Supreme Court.

When the original count had Bush winning by a narrow margin, Vice President Gore decided to try to win by cherry picking votes in three Democrat districts. He not only asked for a recount but an illegal change in the rules based on the Fourteenth Amendment's "Equal Protection Clause." The rules for punch card ballots were posted on the walls of the voting places. They said that the voter was responsible for making sure that there were no hanging chads on their ballots. Ballots with hanging chads would not be counted. However, claiming that every vote must count, teams of workers studied every ballot trying to guess how the voter had intended to vote, even to the point of claiming a vote with the slightest dent in the chad might have meant an intended vote for Gore.

Blame has been shared by butterfly ballots, punch card ballots, hanging chads, dimpled chads, the Republican state administration, racial discrimination, the US Supreme Court, and many more excuses. In fact the entire blame rests on the liberal activist Florida Supreme Court that voted unanimously to illegally change Florida election law after the election as described in more detail in Chapter 2.

Consider what would have happened if the Florida Supreme Court had simply followed the law. On November 14th Katherine Harris would have certified the election of G. W. Bush. By then the Gore team would have known that there were not enough votes in three counties to give Gore the election with standard counting procedures. They would also know that there were probably not enough votes using other methods. The only reasonable course of action would be to ask for a complete recount of the state. Without any other court decisions to bias the local judge, he/she would probably have established a uniform counting procedure for the recount. Based on a recount conducted by a consortium of newspapers that examined the ballots we know now that Bush would still have been elected, but it would have been with the fair recount of the entire state that everyone claimed to want and the people deserved.

The out of control activist extremists on the Florida Supreme Court stole everyone's Constitutional right to a fair election. They changed the certification date From November 14 to November 26 to give the counters more time and changed a few other rules to help Gore. Their error was so obvious that the entire US Supreme Court ruled unanimously that they had exceeded their authority and changed the law. Even the most extreme left wing judges felt compelled to side with the majority.

The U.S Supreme Court sent the case back to the Florida Supreme Court to fix but they only made the matter worse. And finally on December 8 they ordered a statewide recount of all the votes despite a December 12 deadline for the state to complete the election.

"Substantive Equal Protection" Strikes Back

When the final appeal reached the Supreme Court Justices, they ruled 7 to 2 that the "Equal Protection Clause" of the 14th Amendment required that all counties be counted using the same method. Under original understanding this would have been a real stretch, but under the liberal activist doctrine of "Substantive Equal Protection" it is a totally valid decision. Under "Substantive Equal Protection" judges can give any substance/meaning to equal protection they want. And liberal activist judges had already applied substantive equal protection to voting rights with the doctrine of one man one vote that forced the states to redistrict and change the way they voted for state senators. Humorously, only the most liberal justices voted against their own precedent on purely political grounds. If conservatives decided the election, it was with law written by liberal activist judges. It was, however, still an unconstitutional decision based on the "Substantive Equal Protection" fraud.

The five to four vote so often mentioned in the media was not the vote on the law mentioned above but the vote on the remedy. On December 9 the Court ruled 5–4 that no constitutionally valid recount could be completed by the December 12 deadline. The four dissenting Justices wanted the recount to continue under uniform guidelines to be established by the Florida Supreme Court.

It is interesting to note that they could probably have based the decision on legitimate law. The counties had the right to decide how votes were counted and many had posted rules saying that ballots with hanging chads would not be counted. Additionally so many ballots had been handled by so many people that, even if there had been time, there was no way an honest count could possibly have been made. The closest possible thing to a uniform count possible before the deadline was the original count and the Court could have so ruled.

During testimony before the US Supreme Court Justice Stevens asked Mr. Boies, Gore's lawyer, "Could the Florida legislature have done what the (Florida) Supreme Court did?" Boies replied "I think that it would be unusual. I haven't really thought of that question. I think they probably could not." And he also said "Except what I'm saying, Your Honor, is that it wasn't doing exactly the same thing because it wasn't passing a new law. It was interpreting an existing law."

Courts rewrite laws on such a regular basis that the Vice President and some of the nation's top lawyers didn't even consider that it would have been a change of the law if done by a legislature. It's just another way of saying that, in today's court system; if you find a willing judge then the "Letter of the Law" doesn't really matter.

CHAPTER 25. – ONE HELLER OF A DECISION OR ONE JUSTICE AWAY FROM GUN BANS

"This year will go down in history! For the first time, a civilized nation has full gun registration! Our streets will be safer, our police more efficient, and the world will follow our lead into the future!" - Nice sounding quote by an unknown author and falsely attributed to Adolf Hitler.

In 1939 United States v. Miller involved a criminal prosecution under the National Firearms Act of 1934. The Court ruled that a sawed off shotgun could be regulated by the US Congress because shotguns were not military weapons. The decision was flawed because shotguns were in fact used widely in the trench warfare of World War I, however the defense never introduced any evidence to that effect.

From 1934 until 2008 the US Supreme Court managed to avoid taking any major cases on the Second Amendment probably to avoid having to admit that there was an individual right to keep and bear arms. That changed with Heller v. DC. In a five to four decision, the Court ruled that the Second Amendment was an individual right rather than a collective right protecting the state and the military. It did however leave open what limits could be placed on the right by the government in the form of "Reasonable Gun Control."

The fraudulent doctrine of Incorporation dictates that only "Fundamental Rights" are worthy of being applied to the states. In McDonald v Chicago the Court, by another five to four vote, ruled that the Second Amendment was a "Fundamental Right" that applied to the states. See chapter 14 for more details.

"The rifle itself has no moral stature, since it has no will of its own. Naturally, it may be used by evil men for evil purposes, but there are more good men than evil, and while the latter cannot be persuaded to the path of righteousness by propaganda, they can certainly be corrected by good men with rifles." - Jeff Cooper, Art of the Rifle

The point of this chapter is not the Second Amendment rulings but the political and judicial philosophies of the justices who participated in the decisions. The danger is that it would only take one more anti-gun vote to overturn both of these decisions or to rule that virtually all gun control schemes are constitutional.

In the Heller decision current Justices Ginsberg and Breyer join with Stephens in saying "Specifically, there is no indication that the Framers of the Amendment intended to enshrine the common-law right of self-defense in the Constitution." They also stated "The opinion the Court announces today fails to identify any new evidence supporting the view that the Amendment was intended to limit the power of Congress to regulate civilian uses of weapons." In Breyer's dissent Ginsberg agreed "that the Second Amendment protects militia-related, not self-defense-related, interests." There is no mistaking their animus to an honest interpretation of the Second Amendment.

These two justices have a long history as extreme left wing liberal Justices who have little or no regard for the text of either the law or the Constitution except to the degree that they can twist the meaning to meet their personal political goals.

In McDonald Justice Sodomayor Joins Breyer and Ginsberg in stating that the Second Amendment "does not include a general right to keep and bear firearms for purposes of private self-defense" and that it does not apply to the States and is not a "Fundamental" right. Sodomayor was the first of Obama's two extreme left wing pro-abortion, anti-Second Amendment Justices.

Elena Kagan became a Supreme Court Justice too late to participate in the above decisions, however when she clerked for Justice Thurgood Marshall, she wrote that the petitioners "sole contention is that the District of Columbia's firearms statutes violate his constitutional right to 'keep and bear arms,' ...I'm not sympathetic."

Ginsberg, Breyer, Sodomayor, and Kagan would overturn Heller and McDonald in a heartbeat if they had one more vote which Obama would love to provide. All four also subscribe to the "Living Constitution", "Substantive Due Process", and "Right of Privacy" frauds.

Unfortunately we do not know where we stand with the rest on any other gun control issue. Justice Kennedy is a flip flopper who stands mid-way between the extreme left wing of the Court and its more moderate wing. He voted for the "Individual Right" but he is just as likely to support oppressive gun control as oppose it.

Likewise we do not know where the other four stand on the issue of "Reasonable Gun Control" either. In the Heller majority summary it reads: "Like most rights, the Second Amendment right is not unlimited. It is not a right to keep and carry any weapon whatsoever in any manner whatsoever and for whatever purpose: For example, concealed weapons prohibitions have been upheld under the Amendment or state analogues. The Court's opinion should not be taken to cast doubt on longstanding prohibitions on the possession of firearms by felons and the mentally ill, or laws forbidding the carrying of firearms in sensitive places such as schools and government buildings, or laws imposing conditions and qualifications on the commercial sale of arms. Miller's holding that the sorts of weapons protected are those "in common use at the time" finds support in the historical tradition of prohibiting the carrying of dangerous and unusual weapons."

In a 2012 Fox News interview Scalia refused to answer the question regarding what types of guns were protected by the Second Amendment.

The only sure conclusion we can reach is that the addition of one more anti-gun Justice by Obama or one of his successors would probably spell the end of the Second Amendment as an "Individual Right."

"A constitutional guarantee subject to future judges' assessments of its usefulness is no constitutional guarantee at all." - Antonin Scalia

CHAPTER 26. - OBAMACARE OR HOW CHIEF JUSTICE ROBERTS PROVED HE IS A BETTER POLITICIAN THAN JUSTICE

"You can't call a penalty a pig." – Antonin Scalia

The NATIONAL FEDERATION OF INDEPENDENTBUSINESS ET AL. v. SEBELIUS, SECRETARY OF HEALTH AND HUMAN SERVICES, ET AL. known as the ObamaCare decision placed the usually moderate Chief Justice Roberts in the delicate position of giving an honest rendition of the Constitution or buying into Obama's claim that overturning the law would be bad public relations for the Court. Unfortunately he joined the far left wing of the Court in upholding the individual mandate while purportedly returning some small semblance of honesty to the "Commerce Clause." He upheld the Court's integrity by proving yet again that it has little to none.

Robert's opinion ruled that the Anti-Injunction Act, which says you can't have a lawsuit about a tax until someone pays the tax, does not apply to a "Penalty" so the Court can hear the case. He would later rule that the exact same "Penalty" was a tax.

He ruled that the Individual Mandate to purchase insurance was invalid under the "Commerce Clause" because; "Construing the Commerce Clause to permit Congress to regulate individuals precisely because they are doing nothing would open a new and potentially vast domain to congressional authority." And "The Framers knew the difference between doing something and doing nothing. They gave Congress the power to regulate commerce, not to compel it." That he got the extreme left wing of the Court to agree is at least a small victory for honesty.

But then he decided that mandate was Constitutional if you called it a Tax. Because "every reasonable construction must be resorted to, in order to save a statute from unconstitutionality, ...the question is whether it is "fairly possible" to interpret the mandate as imposing such a tax, …The payment is not so high that there is really no choice but to buy health insurance; the payment is not limited to willful violations, as penalties for unlawful acts often are; and the payment is collected solely by the IRS through the normal means of taxation." And so the penalty becomes "a pig" and the Court resorts to "fairly possible" as yet another set of weasel words to excuse the inexcusable.

Scalia, joined by Alito, Kennedy, and Thomas, doesn't mince words in his dissent. "Our cases establish a clear line between a tax and a penalty: "'[A] tax is an enforced contribution to provide for the support of government; a penalty … is an exaction imposed by statute as punishment for an unlawful act.'" He adds that "In a few cases, this Court has held that a "tax" imposed upon private conduct was so onerous as to be in effect a penalty. But we have never held—never—that a penalty imposed for violation of the law was so trivial as to be in effect a tax. We have never held that any exaction imposed for violation of the law is an exercise of Congress' taxing power—even when the statute calls it a tax, much less when (as here) the statute repeatedly calls it a penalty."

Roberts "concluded in Part IV that the Medicaid expansion violates the Constitution by threatening States with the loss of their existing Medicaid funding if they decline to comply with the expansion. The Spending Clause grants Congress the power "to pay the Debts and provide for the … general Welfare of the United States…. Congress may use this power to establish cooperative state-federal Spending Clause programs. The legitimacy of Spending Clause legislation, however, depends on whether a State voluntarily and knowingly accepts the terms of such programs." In this way he determined that states could not be penalized for not accepting the Medicaid expansion.

He saves the rest of the law by saying "The constitutional violation is fully remedied by precluding the Secretary from applying §1396c to withdraw existing Medicaid funds for failure to comply with the requirements set out in the expansion. See §1303. The other provisions of the Affordable Care Act are not affected."

The dissenters agreed that the Medicare mandate was unconstitutional but reached an entirely different conclusion on severability. "The reality that States were given no real choice but to expand Medicaid was not an accident. Congress assumed States would have no choice, and the ACA depends on States' having no choice, because its Mandate requires low-income individuals to obtain insurance many of them can afford only through the Medicaid Expansion. Furthermore, a State's withdrawal might subject everyone in the State to much higher insurance premiums. That is because the Medicaid Expansion will no longer offset the cost to the insurance industry imposed by the ACA's insurance regulations and taxes."

"The two pillars of the Act are the Individual Mandate and the expansion of coverage under Medicaid. In our view, both these central provisions of the Act—the Individual Mandate and Medicaid Expansion—are invalid. It follows, as some of the parties urge, that all other provisions of the Act must fall as well."

The Constitution was written to limit the power of the Federal Government. The Court majority allowed that government to unconstitutionally take over one sixth of the US economy. Honest Justices would have reached a different decision, but five were without honor on June 28, 2012.

"I believe there are more instances of the abridgment of the freedom of the people by gradual and silent encroachments of those in power than by violent and sudden usurpations." - James Madison

"I love my country, not my government." - Jesse Ventura

Missed Opportunity

Article 1, Section 7 of the Constitution states, "All Bills for raising Revenue shall originate in the House of Representatives; but the Senate may propose or concur with Amendments as on other Bills."

ObamaCare was over 2,600 pages of new legislation written entirely in the Senate. It pretended to meet the above requirement by claiming to be an Amendment to a six page bill on an entirely unrelated topic that had passed the House nine months before.

The Merriam-Webster online dictionary defines Amendment as:

"1: the act of amending : correction

2: a material (as compost or sand) that aids plant growth indirectly by improving the condition of the soil

3 a : the process of amending by parliamentary or constitutional procedure

b : an alteration proposed or effected by this process <a constitutional amendment>"

An amendment is a change or an alteration of something that already exists. This bill did not exist until it was written in the Senate.

No reasonable person would consider what the Senate did to be in any way what the Founders would have considered a legitimate amendment of a law. Unfortunately the courts have allowed this type of fraud to stand for so long that no one even considered filing suit on the one provision under which the entirety of ObamaCare was unquestionably unconstitutional.

CHAPTER 27. - MY OWN ADVENTURES OR SOMETIMES IT'S MORE IMPORTANT TO HIRE A LAWYER WHO KNOWS THE JUDGE RATHER THAN THE LAW

Back in the 90's when I got divorced the Judge ordered my ex-wife to assume ownership of a joint credit card with a balance of around $6,000. She was to remove my name from the card. Instead she paid it down a little and then declared bankruptcy leaving me stuck with the $5,000 balance.

The bankruptcy law at the time was very clear. Unless a debt was listed in the filing it was not removed by the bankruptcy. The $5,000 owed me was not listed. In fact it was not actually owed me until the bankruptcy was completed. Therefore under the "Letter of the Law" she owed me $5,000 dollars so I hired a lawyer and sued her for the money in Jay County Court.

The Judge decided that he wanted my lawyer to file a brief which included some precedents on what I was trying to do. Unfortunately the brief I paid for didn't include any good precedents. My lawyer found those months later after it was too late. As a result the Judge decided to put the case on hold until the bankruptcy court made a ruling.

So I was off to another city to find a new lawyer. My old one charged by the hour including driving time and it would have cost me more than I could afford just in travel time to the bankruptcy court at $100 per hour.

At my first free consultation the lawyer looked up the law and told me I had a great case that he would be glad to handle for a $1000 retainer. That was after I told him where to find the law in the U.S. Code.

The next two consultations were totally different. Both lawyers had practiced regularly before the bankruptcy judge in the district. They told me that in similar cases the federal judge had always ruled against the law, because if he didn't there was a good chance that the person with the bankruptcy would file to reopen the case and add the new bill to the filing.

This would add to the court's already heavy case load.

And so even a little guy making under $25,000 a year can become a victim of the imperial judiciary. I dropped the case I had no chance to win and paid the $5,000 credit card bill my ex-wife owed me under the law and the legal fees I owed for my attempt to get justice under the "Rule of Law." If I had continued, the legal fees for losing could have been as much as my ex-wife already owed me.

"It is more important to hire a lawyer who knows the judge than to get one who knows the law." – Stephen Erwin, Founder Jay County Indiana TEA Party

"That's the argument of flexibility and it goes something like this: The Constitution is over 200 years old and societies change. It has to change with society, like a living organism, or it will become brittle and break.... But you would have to be an idiot to believe that," Scalia said. "The Constitution is not a living organism, it is a legal document. It says something and doesn't say other things."

CHAPTER 28. – SUGGESTED SOLUTIONS OR THE TRUTH CAN SET YOU FREE

"I know no safe depository of the ultimate powers of the society but the people themselves; and if we think them not enlightened enough to exercise their control with a wholesome discretion, the remedy is not to take it from them but to inform their discretion by education. This is the true corrective of abuses of Constitutional power." - Thomas Jefferson

In our first chapter, Jefferson told us that the Court was the least dangerous branch of government because it could not write laws or enforce its decisions.

Judge Bork tells us that "it is the Court's vulnerability that makes it invulnerable." And that its "power lies in the fact that the American people choose to obey even its most indefensible mandates rather than contemplate the Alternative."

Many have tried to find a solution to the fraudulent decisions of the Court (or to undo honest ones), but few have had much success. Jefferson tried impeachment; Andrew Jackson simply ignored the Court as did Lincoln; Congress tried to pass a constitutional amendment that would allow two thirds of Congress to override the court; and Roosevelt tried to pack the Court.

Judge Bork's proposed solution "is the formation of a consensus about how judges should behave, a consensus which, by its intellectual and moral force, disciplines those who are subject, and properly so, to no other discipline."

I submit that until we change the dialogue about the Court to one which speaks the truth about its actions and decisions we can't even begin to work on building Judge Bork's consensus.

These truths should be self-evident to any honest person hearing the facts:

1. The only moderate, centrist, impartial, neutral, honest position on the law/Constitution is that it means what it says.

2. We do not have a Conservative Court. It has moved from Extreme Left Wing Activist in the second half of the twentieth century to Moderately Left Wing now.

3. Even the most honest Justice, Clearance Thomas, is left of the Letter of the Law.

4. The Choice of Judicial Nominees is not between left and right. It is between **HONEST and DISHONEST**; "The Rule of Law" or the The Rule of Politically Correct Judges.

5. Until the Court returns to the Center and "The Rule of Law" it has no integrity and deserves no respect.

6. Until the Court admits and corrects the Frauds it has perpetrated on "We the People" it has no integrity and deserves no respect.

7. Ginsberg, Sodomayor, Breyer, and Kagan are political hacks whose only legal talent is writing legal sounding reasons for ignoring the law/Constitution.

8. It is absurd that the left can get away with saying that it is extreme to believe the law actually means what it says.

9. If laws don't mean what they say then they have no meaning at all and Congress is irrelevant.

10. The democrats in the Senate argue about every word in a law and then vote to confirm judges who ignore those same words. This would seem to be the ultimate exercise in stupidity, except that they are politicians.

11. Judges take an Oath to Protect and Defend the Constitution, not precedents; therefore Judges who put precedent, even Supreme Court precedent, before the Constitution are in violation of their oath.

12. Abortion is not settled law. As proof we offer the abject fear of the left that it might be overturned.

"The most brilliant propagandist technique will yield no success unless one fundamental principle is borne in mind constantly - it must confine itself to a few points and repeat them over and over . . . Think of the press as a great keyboard on which the government can play."-- Joseph Goebbels

The point we must repeat over and over is the choice between Honest and Dishonest Justices and Judges.

"We the people are the rightful masters of both Congress and the courts, not to overthrow the Constitution but to overthrow the men who pervert the Constitution." — Abraham Lincoln

The Judicial Accountability Amendment

The "Rule of Law" being the basis of our Republic, judges shall be bound first and foremost by the "Letter of the Law" and by the "Original Understanding" of that law as it can best be determined. Any action that a reasonable person would consider a change of the law if done by a legislature is reserved to the legislature.

This constitutional amendment or one similar should be proposed immediately before Congress. Whether it passed or not the debate would inform the people about the true nature of the Court and increase pressure on the Court to give us honest decisions.

However, if future courts are bound by this Amendment to place "Original Understanding" before precedent, then a Supreme Court which violates the Constitution or the law would find itself constantly plagued by correct lower court decisions challenging their precedent. This would be played out in the press and make it both difficult and embarrassing for justices to avoid the truth or invent new excuses for changing the law. It would provide a new recourse for judges of integrity, and it would provide a legitimate way for the courts to police themselves.

Judges were granted lifetime tenure to guarantee political neutrality. The only truly neutral position on our Constitution and our laws is their original meaning. When Judges place political correctness above the law there is no law. When we are governed by the whims of men there is no true justice.

President George W. Bush stated in May, 2003 that "The judicial confirmation process is broken and it must be fixed." In fact the process will never be fixed as long as the Courts are perceived as political and they will be perceived as political as long as they act politically.

"The strength of the Constitution lies entirely in the determination of each citizen to defend it. Only if every single citizen feels duty bound to do his share in this defense are the constitutional rights secure." — Albert Einstein

The Truth Will Give Us the Strength to Resist

In 1798 the 5th Congress passed the Alien and Sedition Acts which essentially made it illegal for the Democratic-Republican Party to criticize the Adams administration. Jefferson and Madison fathered the Kentucky and Virginia Resolutions of 1798 and 1799 in which the state legislatures took the position that the Alien and Sedition Acts were unconstitutional. "whensoever the general government assumes undelegated powers, its acts are unauthoritative, void, and of no force." It was a constitutional crisis which was resolved by the election, but a little over sixty years later a similar crisis ignited the Civil War. Our Founding Fathers had the political will to stand up and do what was right.

Each of the other branches of the federal government and the states are part of the system of checks and balances set up by the Founding Fathers and each can refuse to obey unconstitutional laws if they have the political will to do so. Our only hope of finding that will is to make sure that everyone in the United States understands the truths about the Supreme Court listed above.

Some say that the Civil War settled the idea of States refusing to obey Federal Laws. But that is only true on an issue that one or both sides are willing to go to war over. Short of that a state refusing unconstitutional federal mandates is an entirely defensible way to challenge the Federal Courts.

In Federalist No. 45, Madison explained: "The powers delegated by the proposed Constitution to the federal government are few and defined. Those which are to remain in the State governments are numerous and indefinite."

Only an honest Court can return a constitutionally limited federal government to "We The People."

Jury Nullification

Juries have the right under the Constitution to rule on the law as well as the facts in a case. Most Judges these days try to hide that fact from juries. If "We the People" would make sure that all juries know of their rights it could alter the balance of power back in the direction of the people where it belongs.

It would in fact be the most powerful tool we could use against the tyranny of the majority that is destroying our Constitutional Republic.

"I consider trial by jury as the only anchor yet imagined by man by which a government can be held to the principles of its Constitution.... It is left therefore, to the juries, if they think the permanent judges are under any bias whatever in any cause, to take on themselves to judge the law as well as the fact." - Thomas Jefferson

The Seventh Amendment Reads "In Suits at common law, where the value in controversy shall exceed twenty dollars, the right of trial by jury shall be preserved, and no fact tried by a jury, shall be otherwise re-examined in any Court of the United States, than according to the rules of the common law."

Unfortunately the $20 amount has never been indexed, just unconstitutionally ignored. The Amendment has never been incorporated so it does not apply to the states since the Court apparently does not feel that a jury trial is a "fundamental right". And while colonial judges routinely instructed jurors that they were the ultimate arbiters of both fact and law, modern judges dictate total control over the evidence, law, and facts, instructing the jury as to what the law is and often forbidding the defense to even mention jury nullification.

A Scary Last Resort That Should Never Be Used

Article III Section II of the Constitution says "In all the other Cases before mentioned, the supreme Court shall have appellate jurisdiction, both as to Law and Fact, with such Exceptions, and under such Regulations as the Congress shall make."

Three months before the Oklahoma City bombing Congressman Joe Biden sponsored an Anti-Terrorism bill which allowed Attorney General Janet Reno to name any organization a terrorist organization and any individual a member of that terrorist organization. It included language which said that that determination "was not subject to review by any Court." When I first read it I could not believe it could be legal. As you can see from the above quoted Constitutional reference it is possibly one of the most dangerous sections in the Constitution. Using it to pull the teeth of the Court is another path that could be followed and one that some have proposed. On the other hand the Court could probably make up a lie about why that Section of the Constitution doesn't actually apply. It is also one that could be very dangerous in the hands of unscrupulous politicians.

These Words Must Have Real Meaning Again In All Branches Of Government.

"I, _____, do solemnly swear (or affirm) that I will support and defend the Constitution of the United States against all enemies, foreign and domestic; that I will bear true faith and allegiance to the same; that I take this obligation freely, without any mental reservation or purpose of evasion; and that I will well and faithfully discharge the duties of the office on which I am about to enter. So help me God."

"Now this is not the end. It is not even the beginning of the end. But it is, perhaps, the end of the beginning." Winston Churchill after the battle of El Alamein 11/10/1942

This is only the end of the beginning because past abuses of the Court are nearly as numerous as the leaves on the trees and our current court is a gift that only keeps on giving. In future books I will explore more of the judicial inventions of the elitist left and further explain the need for and justification of nullification by the states and jury nullification.

APPENDIX A
THE GREAT GUN CONTROL FRAUD - "ASSAULT WEAPONS"

In the 1960s the anti-gun lobby made great gains with the Gun Control Act of 1968 which placed many new restrictions on the sale of firearms. However, the anti-gunners soon ran into a brick wall with their efforts to ban "Saturday Night Specials" defined in the media as cheap, easily concealed handguns and in Congress as any handgun with a short barrel and under a certain weight regardless of quality or price. It would have banned the most popular self-defense handguns of the day.

They then decided to start a campaign to systematically trash the NRA by writing laws that the NRA could not agree to.

Teflon coated handgun bullets that were supposed to penetrate a bullet proof vest a little easier than a normal handgun bullet and which were only sold to law enforcement were dubbed "Cop Killer Bullets" because some of the bullets might get into the hands of crooks and be used against police. Legislation was introduced which included many of the most popular solid core rifle bullets used in hunting and which were never part of the official controversy. The NRA was called anti-police, but we will never know how many police were killed because of a one year education campaign that taught bad guys they needed to shoot police officers in the head because they wear vests. The bill passed when the Democrats removed the rifle bullets from the ban.

When an Austrian firm invented a gun with a polymer frame then Representative Joe Biden was on the air calling for a ban on "all plastic terrorist handguns only good for hijacking airplanes." The gun contained nearly a pound of steel but that didn't matter. The NRA was now helping terrorists. The bill finally passed Congress when it was amended to only ban guns that were all plastic of which none have ever existed. The Glock handgun Biden wanted to ban has never been used to hijack an airplane and is now the most popular law enforcement handgun in the Country because of its advanced safety features, ergonomics, and large capacity magazines. (An all plastic gun made in 2013 on a 3D printer is a piece of junk that blows up after a few shots, is very large with over a 2" diameter barrel, and requires a metal firing pin.)

With the NRA now branded as anti-police and pro-terrorist, Gun Control Incorporated (Now the Brady Campaign) with the help of the media, Clinton, Schumer, Biden, and Feinstein invented an entirely new type of firearm, the "Assault Weapon."

An "Assault Rifle" is a low power personal machine gun used by the military to make the enemy keep their heads down and not return fire when attacking an enemy position. It can then be set to semi-auto fire (one shot per trigger pull) for acute shooting. Civilian firearms are semi-auto only (one shot per trigger pull).

The new "Assault Weapon" was any semi-auto rifle which could hold more than ten bullets in its magazine and which had any of two cosmetic features including pistol grip, bayonet lug, flash suppressor, and adjustable length stock. It is interesting to note that no one has ever been killed by any of these four items unless they were beaten over the head with the gun. Sixteen specific guns were banned including the AK47 semi-auto and the Colt AR-15 Semi-Auto.

The bill also banned all new magazines that held more than ten bullets. This effectively banned the manufacture of all of the most popular self-defense semi-auto handguns. Somehow these geniuses concluded that if someone is shooting at you you should never need more than ten bullets to defend yourself or your family.

These guns were damned in the media as the "Weapon of Choice of Drug Dealers". The NRA correctly pointed out that these guns were rarely used in crime, but for over a year the drum beat in the media never let up. ABC, CBS, NBC, and CNN routinely attacked these guns and virtually every story they did featured dishonest video of someone shooting an AK-47 "Machine Gun" instead of the Semi-Automatic (one shot per trigger pull) they were trying to ban.

But what really makes this law a fraud is that it only banned the manufacture of new weapons so not one single gun was taken off of the street.

And the law of unintended consequences added to the insanity. So many AK-47 style semi-auto rifles were imported in the year before the ban that the market was glutted, prices fell by 66%, and guns that sold for $600 a year before were going for under $200. Thirty round magazines that had been $30 were now selling for $4.95 and millions were imported. When these guns ran out they simply made new ones without bayonet lugs or pistol grips, and sold them with a legal 30 round magazine. Ten years after the ban went into effect you could still buy an AK in any gun store in the US for less than it cost in 1993.

AR-15s also did well. They were renamed and around 900,000 new guns were sold without bayonet lug, flash suppressor, adjustable stock, or 20 round magazine.

Despite the large increase in ownership of these guns they were never a crime problem again until the ban was about to expire. In fact, as soon as the press stopped advertising them as the "Weapon of Choice of Drug Dealers" the already low rate of crime with these guns dropped by over 60%.

And so the "ban" that actually increased ownership of "Assault Weapons" goes down in history as a success that reduced crime.

In 2004 our genius future vice president Joe Biden was all over the airways again telling us that there would be a bloodbath if we put these guns back on the street. Apparently someone forgot to tell him or the major media that they had never been taken off of the street. You would think someone who worked so hard to pass the bill would have understood what was in it.

The ban expired in 2004 because ten years of statistics proved that these guns were in fact rarely used in crime and because the 1993 ban cost the Democrats control of Congress.

In the 19 years since they started this fraudulent campaign I have only heard of one mass murder with an AR-15 style rifle and none with the AK style semi-auto. And yet the call for a new "Assault Weapons" ban was started again in 2012.

The new bill would have banned virtually all new semi-auto firearms and required all existing guns to be taxed and registered with the BATF. The bill was soundly defeated in the Democrat controlled Senate.

APPENDIX B
THE REVOLT OF THE INDIANA TEA PARTIES –
ELITIST SENATOR LUGAR DETHRONED

This story actually begins in 2009 when Blue Dog Democratic Senator Evan Bayh announced that he would not run for a third term. His excuse was that the atmosphere in Congress had become so divisive that he decided to retire. I believe he had the common sense to see the writing on the wall. With the rise of the TEA Party movement he knew that it would be impossible to hide his liberal record and maintain the illusion that he was a moderate democrat. If he wanted any future in politics it was important for him not to get kicked out of the Senate.

To help him along I had been running the website www.ByeByeBayh.com for nearly a year. The sole purpose of that website was to expose Bayh's liberal voting record.

The field of Republican candidates grew quickly. There was former US Representative John Hostettler, State Senator Marlin Stutzman, two TEA Party Candidates, and the anti-gun, big spending, carpet-bagging, Virginia lobbyist, and Republican Central Committee candidate, former Indiana Senator Dan Coates.

With the conservative vote split between four good candidates the worst candidate won by a small margin. Fortunately he has had a much more conservative record in the Senate this time. Many now believe that his earlier liberal votes were influenced by his liberal mentor Senator Richard Lugar.

Everyone had assumed that six term Senator Richard Lugar would retire because he would be 80 years old by the time he was elected to a seventh term. But in December 2010 he announced that he would run for re-election. By the end of the month I had www.RetireLugar2012.com up and running. The purpose of the site was to expose Lugar's liberal voting record which in some areas was even to the left of Evan Bayh's.

Lugar had been a great Reagan Republican when elected, but by 1993 he was a champion of liberal gun ban schemes. He helped Dole shove the fraudulent "Assault Weapons" ban through the US Senate. And he worked hard to get Ruth Bader Ginsberg confirmed to the Supreme Court. Back home in Indiana most Hoosiers were blissfully unaware of Lugar's liberal transformation because it had been so long since he had a real challenger. But by 2010 his votes for Supreme Court Justices Sodomayor and Kagan, along with his sponsorship of the Dream Act, resulted in many more people becoming aware of his real positions on the issues.

"Senator Lugar is a big spending Washington insider who has repeatedly voted for gun bans, Cap and Trade, amnesty for illegal Immigrants, and extreme left wing Supreme Court Justices." – Stephen Erwin on TEA Party flyers and e-mails.

By then Hoosiers for a Conservative Senate had already been founded to work for Liberal Lugar's defeat. Founders Monica Boyer (Kosciusko County Silent NO More) and Greg Fettig (Indianapolis TEA Party) traveled to Washington to talk to the Senator on the issues that December. Monica reported that "Lugar basically told us how it was. There was no discussion and he didn't hear us."

On 1/26/11 US News and World Report quoted Senator Lugar insulting the Tea Party saying they use "large cliché' titles, but are not able to articulate specifics." The far left finds every conservative opinion ignorant, but we don't expect that kind of condescending rhetoric from our own party's elder statesman. Calling his base inarticulate is tantamount to admitting he just didn't care enough to listen to his party's conservative base. After 35 years of living in Washington he apparently thought he was smarter than the average Hoosier.

In another statement Lugar urged the tea party to "get real" about the START treaty. And on WANE TV he said "I hear Tea Party or other people talking about they were against START. I said 'Well, now, hang on here,' If you want to get into START, let's talk about it, but realistically as Americans, not as some Republican renegade."

Hoosiers for a Conservative Senate invited all of the TEA Party leaders in the State to meet and plan Lugar's defeat. The main goal was not to repeat the 2010 mistake of fielding four conservative candidates. If even two split the vote in the primary it would guarantee a Lugar win.

Most of the state's TEA Parties sent representatives. The group decided to have a convention in the fall to pick their candidate for the Senate. Since many TEA Parties were 501C3 they could not officially endorse a candidate. That was only one of the problems that the groups would need to address.

Given that there were over on hundred independent groups in Indiana, the biggest mistake that HFCS made was to alienate some of the groups by appearing to act as the official spokespersons for all of the TEA Parties. This was more a matter of the press taking the easy way out and calling the people who had been mentioned in the media. It is, however, a pitfall that other states need to try and avoid.

Several groups formed separate umbrella groups that were not a 501c3 so that their members could join if they wanted to belong to a group that officially endorsed a candidate. Others chose to remain as educational groups only while their members worked for the candidate of their choice which soon became Richard Mourdock.

In February Indiana State Treasurer Richard Mourdock announced his candidacy for Lugar's Senate seat. It had been members of the Indiana Republican Central Committee who had asked him to consider running. Before he accepted the challenge he polled the Republican party chairmen who overwhelmingly gave him their support. "Almost three quarters of the Republican county chairs say it's time to dump Dick Lugar and to me that's the real story here," Mourdock told CNN. Many of the chairman cited the fact that they had not seen the Senator in their county for years as the reason they supported Mourdock.

TEA Party activists all across the state went to work for Mourdock marching in parades, working tables at County Fairs and gun shows, passing out flyers, and writing Letters to the Editor endorsing Mourdock and exposing Lugar's record. During this time Club for Growth did a media buy on Lugar's record. I spent the summer working as a volunteer for the Mourdock Campaign before resigning to start a statewide letter writing campaign and becoming the sixth district representative for Hoosiers for a Conservative Senate.

Indiana state representative, Mike Delph, had considered running. A large percentage of TEA Party members across the state made it clear that if he chose to run and split the vote he would get absolutely no TEA Party support. He decided that he would not run.

By the October HFCS Convention Mourdock had around 67% name recognition and was only down around ten percent. Tea Party groups sent representatives who voted their personal choice and not the official choice of their group. That way none of the 501c3 groups were making an official endorsement which would have endangered their tax exempt status. Over 90 groups sent members and Richard Lugar received exactly one vote.

Freedom works officially endorsed Richard Mourdock and soon other endorsements and money for the campaign started coming in. The TEA Party had pushed the Mourdock campaign to the point where his candidacy was no longer an impossible dream but a solid challenge to an entrenched incumbent and the RNC.

Lugar's advertising and brochures, which had already been disingenuous, turned extremely dirty as the elitist Senator began to realize that he might be in trouble. And of course he resorted to the dirtiest trick in the democrat play book, he claimed that his opponent was lying about his record which was in fact the real lie.

Freedom Works supplied Yard Signs, Door Hangers, and a Phone Banking System and the members of TEA Parties around the state went to work.

With help from HFCS a lawsuit was filed challenging Lugar's eligibility to run. The US Constitution requires that a Senator must be a resident in the State when he is elected. Lugar sold his home in Indiana in 1977 and moved to Virginia. The Indiana Constitution is vague about residency and "everybody does it" so the lawsuit failed but the publicity woke up Indiana to the fact that Lugar was an aloof absentee Senator with very little concern about the opinions of his constituents.

The Debate between Mourdock and Lugar proved that Richard could hold his own on the issues with the famous six term Senator who had ceased to be perceived as a "Statesman" due to the exceptionally dirty campaign he was running.

The last nail in his coffin was the mailing from the NRA stating that Lugar had gotten his "F" rating on gun control the hard way, "he earned it."

By the weekend before the primary Mourdock was up slightly in the polls and Lugar was begging Democrats to take a Republican ballot and save his Senate seat.

What no one had expected, except the TEA Party, was the 21% margin of victory by the Mourdock campaign. The wide margin was the difference between Mourdock's energized base and Lugar's base that was luke warm at best.

Here in Jay County, where we started running letters to the editor the week Lugar announced he would run, the margin was 30%.

The Indiana TEA Parties sent a message to Washington; Not a single left leaning big government Republican in Congress is safe no matter how big or famous they are.

I don't believe in the term RINO (Republican In Name Only) because anyone of any persuasion can belong to the party. But we have served notice to those in the Leadership who have abandoned the principles of free market conservatism and the "Rule of Law" set down in the Constitution that **Conservatives are taking back the Grand Old Party of Lincoln and Reagan.**

Unfortunately, while he was leading in the polls before the last debate, Richard Mourdock used an unfortunate choice of words regarding abortion and rape that his opponent twisted and then demagogued into an election win. Like Romney, Mourdock lost because he let his opponent define him without providing a sufficient response to the misinformation spread by a slimy advertising campaign based almost entirely on personal attacks. Mourdock was by far the best choice for Indiana Senator, but a left wing extremist claiming to be a moderate managed to paint a common sense Hoosier as a right wing extremist. In both campaigns left wing sleaze won the day.

APPENDIX C
THE CONSTITUTION OF THE UNITED STATES

We the People of the United States, in Order to form a more perfect Union, establish Justice, insure domestic Tranquility, provide for the common defense, promote the general Welfare, and secure the Blessings of Liberty to ourselves and our Posterity, do ordain and establish this Constitution for the United States of America.

Article I
Section 1

All legislative Powers herein granted shall be vested in a Congress of the United States, which shall consist of a Senate and House of Representatives.

Section 2

1: The House of Representatives shall be composed of Members chosen every second Year by the People of the several States, and the Electors in each State shall have the Qualifications requisite for Electors of the most numerous Branch of the State Legislature.

2: No Person shall be a Representative who shall not have attained to the Age of twenty five Years, and been seven Years a Citizen of the United States, and who shall not, when elected, be an Inhabitant of that State in which he shall be chosen.

3: Representatives and direct Taxes shall be apportioned among the several States which may be included within this Union, according to their respective Numbers, which shall be determined by adding to the whole Number of free Persons, including those bound to Service for a Term of Years, and excluding Indians not taxed, three fifths of all other Persons. The actual Enumeration shall be made within three Years after the first

Meeting of the Congress of the United States, and within every subsequent Term often Years, in such Manner as they shall by Law direct. The Number of Representatives shall not exceed one for every thirty Thousand, but each State shall have at Least one Representative; and until such enumeration shall be made, the State of New Hampshire shall be entitled to chuse three, Massachusetts eight, Rhode-Island and Providence Plantations one, Connecticut five, New-York six, New Jersey four, Pennsylvania eight, Delaware one, Maryland six, Virginia ten, North Carolina five, South Carolina five, and Georgia three.

4: When vacancies happen in the Representation from any State, the Executive Authority thereof shall issue Writs of Election to fill such Vacancies.

5: The House of Representatives shall chuse their Speaker and other Officers; and shall have the sole Power of Impeachment.

Section 3

1: The Senate of the United States shall be composed of two Senators from each State, chosen by the Legislature thereof, for six Years; and each Senator shall have one Vote.

2: Immediately after they shall be assembled in Consequence of the first Election, they shall be divided as equally as may be into three Classes. The Seats of the Senators of the first Class shall be vacated at the Expiration of the second Year, of the second Class at the Expiration of the fourth Year, and of the third Class at the Expiration of the sixth Year, so that one third may be chosen every second Year; and if Vacancies happen by Resignation, or otherwise, during the Recess of the Legislature of any State, the Executive thereof may make temporary Appointments until the next Meeting of the Legislature, which shall then fill such Vacancies.

3: No Person shall be a Senator who shall not have attained to the Age of thirty Years, and been nine Years a Citizen of the United States, and who shall not, when elected, be an Inhabitant of that State for which he shall be chosen.

4: The Vice President of the United States shall be President of the Senate, but shall have no Vote, unless they be equally divided.

5: The Senate shall chuse their other Officers, and also a President pro tempore, in the Absence of the Vice President, or when he shall exercise the Office of President of the United States.

6: The Senate shall have the sole Power to try all Impeachments. When sitting for that Purpose, they shall be on Oath or Affirmation. When the President of the United States is tried, the Chief Justice shall preside: And no Person shall be convicted without the Concurrence of two thirds of the Members present.

7: Judgment in Cases of impeachment shall not extend further than to removal from Office, and disqualification to hold and enjoy any Office of honor, Trust or Profit under the United States: but the Party convicted shall nevertheless be liable and subject to Indictment, Trial, Judgment and Punishment, according to Law.

Section 4

1: The Times, Places and Manner of holding Elections for Senators and Representatives, shall be prescribed in each State by the Legislature thereof; but the Congress may at any time by Law make or alter such Regulations, except as to the Places of chusing Senators.

2: The Congress shall assemble at least once in every Year, and such Meeting shall be on the first Monday in December, unless they shall by Law appoint a different Day.

Section 5

1: Each House shall be the Judge of the Elections, Returns and Qualifications of its own Members, and a Majority of each shall constitute a Quorum to do Business; but a smaller Number may adjourn from day to day, and may be authorized to compel the Attendance of absent Members, in such Manner, and under such Penalties as each House may provide.

2: Each House may determine the Rules of its Proceedings, punish its Members for disorderly Behaviour, and, with the Concurrence of two thirds, expel a Member.

3: Each House shall keep a Journal of its Proceedings, and from time to time publish the same, excepting such Parts as may in their Judgment require Secrecy; and the Yeas and Nays of the Members of either House on any question shall, at the Desire of one fifth of those Present, be entered on the Journal.

4: Neither House, during the Session of Congress, shall, without the Consent of the other, adjourn for more than three days, nor to any other Place than that in which the two Houses shall be sitting.

Section 6

1: The Senators and Representatives shall receive a Compensation for their Services, to be ascertained by Law, and paid out of the Treasury of the United States. They shall in all Cases, except Treason, Felony and Breach of the Peace, be privileged from Arrest during their Attendance at the Session of their respective Houses, and in going to and returning from the same; and for any Speech or Debate in either House, they shall not be questioned in any other Place.

2: No Senator or Representative shall, during the Time for which he was elected, be appointed to any civil Office under the Authority of the United States, which shall have been created, or the Emoluments whereof shall have been encreased during such time; and no Person holding any

Office under the United States, shall be a Member of either House during his Continuance in Office.

Section 7

1: All Bills for raising Revenue shall originate in the House of Representatives; but the Senate may propose or concur with Amendments as on other Bills.

2: Every Bill which shall have passed the House of Representatives and the Senate, shall, before it become a Law, be presented to the President of the United States; If he approve he shall sign it, but if not he shall return it, with his Objections to that House in which it shall have originated, who shall enter the Objections at large on their Journal, and proceed to reconsider it. If after such Reconsideration two thirds of that House shall agree to pass the Bill, it shall be sent, together with the Objections, to the other House, by which it shall likewise be reconsidered, and if approved by two thirds of that House, it shall become a Law. But in all such Cases the Votes of both Houses shall be determined by yeas and Nays, and the Names of the Persons voting for and against the Bill shall be entered on the Journal of each House respectively. If any Bill shall not be returned by the President within ten Days (Sundays excepted) after it shall have been presented to him, the Same shall be a Law, in like Manner as if he had signed it, unless the Congress by their Adjournment prevent its Return, in which Case it shall not be a Law.

3: Every Order, Resolution, or Vote to which the Concurrence of the Senate and House of Representatives may be necessary (except on a question of Adjournment) shall be presented to the President of the United States; and before the Same shall take Effect, shall be approved by him, or being disapproved by him, shall be repassed by two thirds of the Senate and House of Representatives, according to the Rules and Limitations prescribed in the Case of a Bill.

Section 8

1: The Congress shall have Power To lay and collect Taxes, Duties, Imposts and Excises, to pay the Debts and provide for the common Defence and general Welfare of the United States; but all Duties, Imposts and Excises shall be uniform throughout the United States;

2: To borrow Money on the credit of the United States;

3: To regulate Commerce with foreign Nations, and among the several States, and with the Indian Tribes;

4: To establish an uniform Rule of Naturalization, and uniform Laws on the subject of Bankruptcies throughout the United States;

5: To coin Money, regulate the Value thereof, and of foreign Coin, and fix the Standard of Weights and Measures;

6: To provide for the Punishment of counterfeiting the Securities and current Coin of the United States;

7: To establish Post Offices and post Roads;

8: To promote the Progress of Science and useful Arts, by securing for limited Times to Authors and Inventors the exclusive Right to their respective Writings and Discoveries;

9: To constitute Tribunals inferior to the supreme Court;

10: To define and punish Piracies and Felonies committed on the high Seas, and Offences against the Law of Nations;

11: To declare War, grant Letters of Marque and Reprisal, and make Rules concerning Captures on Land and Water;

12: To raise and support Armies, but no Appropriation of Money to that Use shall be for a longer Term than two Years;

13: To provide and maintain a Navy;

14: To make Rules for the Government and Regulation of the land and naval Forces;

15: To provide for calling forth the Militia to execute the Laws of the Union, suppress Insurrections and repel Invasions;

16: To provide for organizing, arming, and disciplining, the Militia, and for governing such Part of them as may be employed in the Service of the United States, reserving to the States respectively, the Appointment of the Officers, and the Authority of training the Militia according to the discipline prescribed by Congress;

17: To exercise exclusive Legislation in all Cases whatsoever, over such District (not exceeding ten Miles square) as may, by Cession of particular States, and the Acceptance of Congress, become the Seat of the Government of the United States, and to exercise like Authority over all Places purchased by the Consent of the Legislature of the State in which the Same shall be, for the Erection of Forts, Magazines, Arsenals, dock-Yards, and other needful Buildings;--And

18: To make all Laws which shall be necessary and proper for carrying into Execution the foregoing Powers, and all other Powers vested by this Constitution in the Government of the United States, or in any Department or Officer thereof.

Section 9

1: The Migration or Importation of such Persons as any of the States now existing shall think proper to admit, shall not be prohibited by the Congress prior to the Year one thousand eight hundred and eight, but a Tax or duty may be imposed on such Importation, not exceeding ten dollars for each Person.

2: The Privilege of the Writ of Habeas Corpus shall not be suspended, unless when in Cases of Rebellion or Invasion the public Safety may require it.

3: No Bill of Attainder or ex post facto Law shall be passed.

4: No Capitation, or other direct, Tax shall be laid, unless in Proportion to the Census or Enumeration herein before directed to be taken.

5: No Tax or Duty shall be laid on Articles exported from any State.

6: No Preference shall be given by any Regulation of Commerce or Revenue to the Ports of one State over those of another: nor shall Vessels bound to, or from, one State, be obliged to enter, clear, or pay Duties in another.

7: No Money shall be drawn from the Treasury, but in Consequence of Appropriations made by Law; and a regular Statement and Account of the Receipts and Expenditures of all public Money shall be published from time to time.

8: No Title of Nobility shall be granted by the United States: And no Person holding any Office of Profit or Trust under them, shall, without the Consent of the Congress, accept of any present, Emolument, Office, or Title, of any kind whatever, from any King, Prince, or foreign State.

Section 10

1: No State shall enter into any Treaty, Alliance, or Confederation; grant Letters of Marque and Reprisal; coin Money; emit Bills of Credit; make any Thing but gold and silver Coin a Tender in Payment of Debts; pass any Bill of Attainder, ex post facto Law, or Law impairing the Obligation of Contracts, or grant any Title of Nobility.

2: No State shall, without the Consent of the Congress, lay any Imposts or Duties on Imports or Exports, except what may be absolutely necessary for executing it's inspection Laws: and the net Produce of all Duties and Imposts, laid by any State on Imports or Exports, shall be for the Use of the Treasury of the United States; and all such Laws shall be subject to the Revision and Controul of the Congress.

3: No State shall, without the Consent of Congress, lay any Duty of Tonnage, keep Troops, or Ships of War in time of Peace, enter into any Agreement or Compact with another State, or with a foreign Power, or engage in War, unless actually invaded, or in such imminent Danger as will not admit of delay.

Article II

Section 1

1: The executive Power shall be vested in a President of the United States of America. He shall hold his Office during the Term of four Years, and, together with the Vice President, chosen for the same Term, be elected, as follows

2: Each State shall appoint, in such Manner as the Legislature thereof may direct, a Number of Electors, equal to the whole Number of Senators and Representatives to which the State may be entitled in the Congress: but no Senator or Representative, or Person holding an Office of Trust or Profit under the United States, shall be appointed an Elector.

3: The Electors shall meet in their respective States, and vote by Ballot for two Persons, of whom one at least shall not be an Inhabitant of the same State with themselves. And they shall make a List of all the Persons voted for, and of the Number of Votes for each; which List they shall sign and certify, and transmit sealed to the Seat of the Government of the United States, directed to the President of the Senate. The President of the Senate shall, in the Presence of the Senate and House of Representatives, open all the Certificates, and the Votes shall then be counted. The Person having the greatest Number of Votes shall be the President, if such Number be a Majority of the whole Number of Electors appointed; and if there be more than one who have such Majority, and have an equal Number of Votes, then the House of Representatives shall immediately chuse by Ballot one of them for President; and if no Person have a Majority, then from the five highest on the List the said House shall in like Mannerchuse the President. But in chusing the President, the Votes shall be taken by States, the Representation from each State having one Vote; A quorum for this Purpose shall consist of a Member or Members from two thirds of the States, and a Majority of all the States shall be necessary to a Choice. In every Case, after the Choice of the President, the Person having the greatest Number of Votes of the Electors shall be the Vice President. But if there should remain two or more who have equal Votes, the Senate shall chuse from them by Ballot the Vice President.

4: The Congress may determine the Time of chusing the Electors, and the Day on which they shall give their Votes; which Day shall be the same throughout the United States.

5: No Person except a natural born Citizen, or a Citizen of the United States, at the time of the Adoption of this Constitution, shall be eligible to the Office of President; neither shall any Person be eligible to that Office who shall not have attained to the Age of thirty five Years, and been fourteen Years a Resident within the United States.

6: In Case of the Removal of the President from Office, or of his Death, Resignation, or Inability to discharge the Powers and Duties of the said Office, the Same shall devolve on the Vice President, and the Congress may by Law provide for the Case of Removal, Death, Resignation or Inability, both of the President and Vice President, declaring what Officer shall then act as President, and such Officer shall act accordingly, until the Disability be removed, or a President shall be elected.

7: The President shall, at stated Times, receive for his Services, a Compensation, which shall neither be encreased nor diminished during the Period for which he shall have been elected, and he shall not receive within that Period any other Emolument from the United States, or any of them.

8: Before he enter on the Execution of his Office, he shall take the following Oath or Affirmation:--"I do solemnly swear (or affirm) that I will faithfully execute the Office of President of the United States, and will to the best of my Ability, preserve, protect and defend the Constitution of the United States."

Section 2

1: The President shall be Commander in Chief of the Army and Navy of the United States, and of the Militia of the several States, when called into the actual Service of the United States; he may require the Opinion, in writing, of the principal Officer in each of the executive Departments, upon any Subject relating to the Duties of their respective Offices, and he shall have Power to grant Reprieves and Pardons for Offences against the United States, except in Cases of Impeachment.

2: He shall have Power, by and with the Advice and Consent of the Senate, to make Treaties, provided two thirds of the Senators present concur; and he shall nominate, and by and with the Advice and Consent of the Senate, shall appoint Ambassadors, other public Ministers and Consuls, Judges of the supreme Court, and all other Officers of the United States, whose Appointments are not herein otherwise provided for, and which shall be established by Law: but the Congress may by Law vest the Appointment of such inferior Officers, as they think proper, in the President alone, in the Courts of Law, or in the Heads of Departments.

3: The President shall have Power to fill up all Vacancies that may happen during the Recess of the Senate, by granting Commissions which shall expire at the End of their next Session.

Section 3

He shall from time to time give to the Congress Information of the State of the Union, and recommend to their Consideration such Measures as he shall judge necessary and expedient; he may, on extraordinary Occasions, convene both Houses, or either of them, and in Case of Disagreement between them, with Respect to the Time of Adjournment, he may adjourn them to such Time as he shall think proper; he shall receive Ambassadors and other public Ministers; he shall take Care that the Laws be faithfully executed, and shall Commission all the Officers of the United States.

Section 4

The President, Vice President and all civil Officers of the United States, shall be removed from Office on Impeachment for, and Conviction of, Treason, Bribery, or other high Crimes and Misdemeanors.

Article III

Section 1

The judicial Power of the United States, shall be vested in one supreme Court, and in such inferior Courts as the Congress may from time to time ordain and establish. The Judges, both of the supreme and inferior Courts, shall hold their Offices during good Behaviour, and shall, at stated Times, receive for their Services, a Compensation, which shall not be diminished during their Continuance in Office.

Section 2

1:   The judicial Power shall extend to all Cases, in Law and Equity, arising under this Constitution, the Laws of the United States, and Treaties made, or which shall be made, under their Authority;--to all Cases affecting Ambassadors, other public Ministers and Consuls;--to all Cases of admiralty and maritime Jurisdiction;--to Controversies to which the United States shall be a Party;--to Controversies between two or more States;--between a State and Citizens of another State. --between Citizens of different States, --between Citizens of the same State claiming Lands under Grants of different States, and between a State, or the Citizens thereof, and foreign States, Citizens or Subjects.

2:   In all Cases affecting Ambassadors, other public Ministers and Consuls, and those in which a State shall be Party, the supreme Court shall have original Jurisdiction. In all the other Cases before mentioned, the supreme Court shall have appellate Jurisdiction, both as to Law and Fact, with such Exceptions, and under such Regulations as the Congress shall make.

3:   The Trial of all Crimes, except in Cases of Impeachment, shall be by Jury; and such Trial shall be held in the State where the said Crimes shall have been committed; but when not committed within any State, the Trial shall be at such Place or Places as the Congress may by Law have directed.

Section 3

1:   Treason against the United States, shall consist only in levying War against them, or in adhering to their Enemies, giving them Aid and Comfort.   No Person shall be convicted of Treason unless on the Testimony of two Witnesses to the same overt Act, or on Confession in open Court.

2:   The Congress shall have Power to declare the Punishment of Treason, but no Attainder of Treason shall work Corruption of Blood, or Forfeiture except during the Life of the Person attainted.

Article IV

Section 1

Full Faith and Credit shall be given in each State to the public Acts, Records, and judicial Proceedings of every other State. And the Congress may by general Laws prescribe the Manner in which such Acts, Records and Proceedings shall be proved, and the Effect thereof.

Section 2

1: The Citizens of each State shall be entitled to all Privileges and Immunities of Citizens in the several States.

2: A Person charged in any State with Treason, Felony, or other Crime, who shall flee from Justice, and be found in another State, shall on Demand of the executive Authority of the State from which he fled, be delivered up, to be removed to the State having Jurisdiction of the Crime.

3: No Person held to Service or Labour in one State, under the Laws thereof, escaping into another, shall, in Consequence of any Law or Regulation therein, be discharged from such Service or Labour, but shall be delivered up on Claim of the Party to whom such Service or Labour may be due1

Section 3

1: New States may be admitted by the Congress into this Union; but no new State shall be formed or erected within the Jurisdiction of any other State; nor any State be formed by the Junction of two or more States, or Parts of States, without the Consent of the Legislatures of the States concerned as well as of the Congress.

2: The Congress shall have Power to dispose of and make all needful Rules and Regulations respecting the Territory or other Property belonging to the United States; and nothing in this Constitution shall be so construed as to Prejudice any Claims of the United States, or of any particular State.

Section 4

The United States shall guarantee to every State in this Union a Republican Form of Government, and shall protect each of them against Invasion; and on Application of the Legislature, or of the Executive (when the Legislature cannot be convened) against domestic Violence.

Article V

The Congress, whenever two thirds of both Houses shall deem it necessary, shall propose Amendments to this Constitution, or, on the Application of the Legislatures of two thirds of the several States, shall call a Convention for proposing Amendments, which, in either Case, shall be valid to all Intents and Purposes, as Part of this Constitution, when ratified by the Legislatures of three fourths of the several States, or by Conventions in three fourths thereof, as the one or the other Mode of Ratification may be proposed by the Congress; Provided that no Amendment which may be made prior to the Year One thousand eight hundred and eight shall in any Manner affect the first and fourth Clauses in the Ninth Section of the first Article; and that no State, without its Consent, shall be deprived of its equal Suffrage in the Senate.

Article VI

1:   All Debts contracted and Engagements entered into, before the Adoption of this Constitution, shall be as valid against the United States under this Constitution, as under the Confederation.

2:   This Constitution, and the Laws of the United States which shall be made in Pursuance thereof; and all Treaties made, or which shall be made, under the Authority of the United States, shall be the supreme Law of the Land; and the Judges in every State shall be bound thereby, any Thing in the Constitution or Laws of any State to the Contrary notwithstanding.

3:   The Senators and Representatives before mentioned, and the Members of the several State Legislatures, and all executive and judicial Officers, both of the United States and of the several States, shall be bound by Oath or Affirmation, to support this Constitution; but no religious Test shall ever be required as a Qualification to any Office or public Trust under the United States.

Article VII

The Ratification of the Conventions of nine States, shall be sufficient for the Establishment of this Constitution between the States so ratifying the Same.

The Word "the", being interlined between the seventh and eight Lines of the first Page, The Word "Thirty" being partly written on an Erazurein the fifteenth Line of the first Page. The Words "is tried" being interlined between the thirty second and thirty third Lines of the first Page and the Word "the" being interlined between the forty third and forty fourth Lines of the second Page.

APPENDIX D
THE BILL OF RIGHTS

Article [I]

Congress shall make no law respecting an establishment of religion, or prohibiting the free exercise thereof; or abridging the freedom of speech, or of the press; or the right of the people peaceably to assemble, and to petition the Government for a redress of grievances.

Article [II]

A well regulated Militia, being necessary to the security of a free State, the right of the people to keep and bear Arms, shall not be infringed.

Article [III]

No Soldier shall, in time of peace be quartered in any house, without the consent of the Owner, nor in time of war, but in a manner to be prescribed by law.

Article [IV]

The right of the people to be secure in their persons, houses, papers, and effects, against unreasonable searches and seizures, shall not be violated, and no Warrants shall issue, but upon probable cause, supported by Oath or affirmation, and particularly describing the place to be searched, and the persons or things to be seized.

Article [V]

No person shall be held to answer for a capital, or otherwise infamous crime, unless on a presentment or indictment of a Grand Jury, except in cases arising in the land or naval forces, or in the Militia, when in actual service in time of War or public danger; nor shall any person be subject for the same offence to be twice put in jeopardy of life or limb; nor shall be compelled in any criminal case to be a witness against himself, nor be deprived of life, liberty, or property, without due process of law; nor shall private property be taken for public use, without just compensation.

Article [VI]

In all criminal prosecutions, the accused shall enjoy the right to a speedy and public trial, by an impartial jury of the State and district wherein the crime shall have been committed, which district shall have been previously ascertained by law, and to be informed of the nature and cause of the accusation; to be confronted with the witnesses against him; to have compulsory process for obtaining witnesses in his favor, and to have the Assistance of Counsel for his defence.

Article [VII]

In Suits at common law, where the value in controversy shall exceed twenty dollars, the right of trial by jury shall be preserved, and no fact tried by a jury, shall be otherwise re-examined in any Court of the United States, than according to the rules of the common law.

Article [VIII]

Excessive bail shall not be required, nor excessive fines imposed, nor cruel and unusual punishments inflicted.

Article [IX]

The enumeration in the Constitution, of certain rights, shall not be construed to deny or disparage others retained by the people.

Article [X]

The powers not delegated to the United States by the Constitution, nor prohibited by it to the States, are reserved to the States respectively, or to the people.

ABOUT THE AUTHOR

Stephen Erwin was born in Fort Wayne Indiana in 1947, survived 12 years of parochial school, and earned a bachelor degree from Butler University in Indianapolis. He taught school for three years before seeking jobs in the private sector.

Steve worked 22 years as an industrial engineer and cost reduction expert. After being downsized out of his job he obtained an associate degree in computer networking with a 4.0 grade point average. He was also rated as a Microsoft Certified Professional. He retired to write this book in 2012.

He has earned a reputation as a constant bane to local and state politicians with over 40 years of practice writing Letters to the Editor.

Steve helped run the successful campaign for Portland Indiana mayor Democrat Vaughn Bailey in the '80s. Vaughn then angered the City Council by appointing Steve, a Republican, to his board of works. Steve later ran an unsuccessful campaign for mayor himself.

Steve was a registered lobbyist to both the U.S. House and Senate where he unsuccessfully lobbied for a Judicial Accountability Amendment.

When Senator Lugar announced that he would run for a seventh term Steve started the website www.RetireLugar2012.com. He also started the Jay County TEA Party and served as sixth district representative to Hoosiers for a Conservative Senate. Steve ran a statewide letter writing campaign to expose Lugar's liberal voting record.

Steve is married and has two children, seven grandchildren, three step-children, and three step-grandchildren. Steve loves computers, photography, target shooting, and irritating politicians.

www.ingramcontent.com/pod-product-compliance
Lightning Source LLC
Chambersburg PA
CBHW030842180526

45163CB00004B/1420